"WE MUST FACE THE SAL THAT A. THE ELEVEN O' CLOCK HOUR ON SUNDAY MORNING WHEN WE STAND TO SING, WE STAND IN THE MOST SEGREGATED HOUR IN AMERICA."

MARTIN LUTHER KING JR.

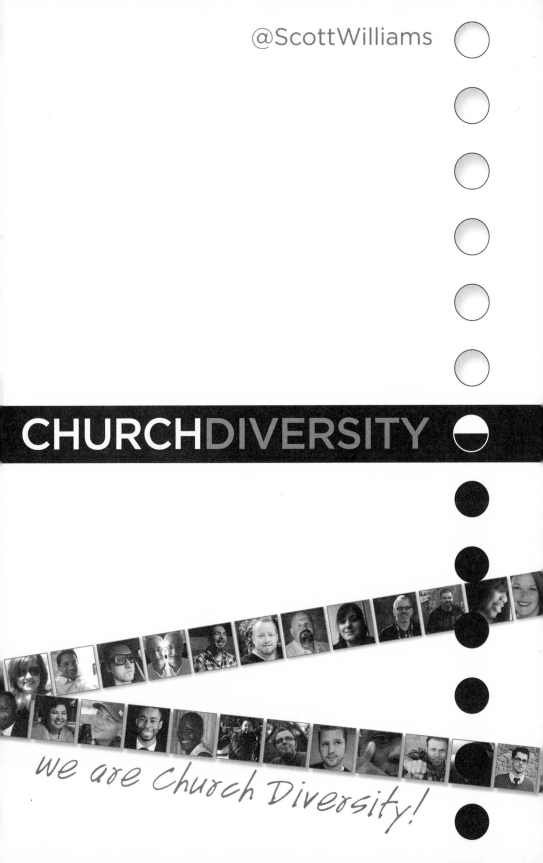

First printing: March 2011

Copyright © 2011 by Scott Williams. All rights reserved. No part of this book may be used or reproduced in any manner whatsoever without written permission of the publisher, except in the case of brief quotations in articles and reviews. For information write:

New Leaf Press, P.O. Box 726, Green Forest, AR 72638

New Leaf Press is a division of the New Leaf Publishing Group, Inc.

ISBN: 978-0-89221-703-8
Library of Congress Number: 2011923687

Cover by Kyle Wiley, Eightdaystudio.com
Photo Credit: Abi Martin, abiruth.com
Book Trailers: Chase Layman, behemothco.com

Unless otherwise noted, Scripture quotations are from the New International Version of the Bible.

Please consider requesting that a copy of this volume
be purchased by your local library system.

Printed in the United States of America

Please visit our website for other great titles:
www.newleafpress.net

For information regarding author interviews,
please contact the publicity department at (870) 438-5288

New Leaf Press
A Division of New Leaf Publishing Group
www.newleafpress.net

What people are saying about *Church Diversity*

Scott Williams is an incredible and insightful leader who understands both the local church and the issue of diversity. He has embraced the intent of the gospel: God redeeming people from every nation through the blood of Christ. I've definitely learned from Scott and this book. You will too.

— Eric Geiger
Author, *Simple Church*
Executive Pastor, Christ Fellowship Miami

Whatever racial woes we face in America, they cannot be dealt with by politicians or Washington, DC, but rather by the local church. Scott's book can help our nation navigate through this critical and much needed conversation on race.

— J.C. Watts Jr.
Former Member of Congress

Diversity of people gives birth to the diversity of thought and bright new ideas emerge. For the sake of the gospel, our churches need these bright new ideas. Scott Williams is a superb communicator who unpacks diversity with courage, passion, and vulnerability.

—Tammy Kelley
Former Senior Leadership Team member
Willow Creek Community Church

Filmmaking is all about experiencing a journey through the eyes of another. Yet, when it comes to integration, this essential gift remains largely misunderstood. Scott Williams is ever seeking to see this gift opened and embraced. His book, like his life and ministry, is an invitation to the most rewarding of all human journeys.

— Jim Hanon,
Writer/Director *End of the Spear*

Leading a diverse congregation takes courage, intentionality, and consistency. Scott takes us to the practical side of theology and teaches HOW to become a church rich with diversity. This is one book every church leader needs to read so that our congregations on earth will start looking more like heaven!

— Troy Gramling
Lead Pastor, Potential Church

The mandate of Jesus spoken in his last words (Acts 1:8) was about multi-ethnicity. The first day of the church was strategic when Jerusalem was crowded with multi-ethnicity (Acts 2:5–11). The first church-wide controversy and conflict was about church diversity and multi-ethnicity (Acts 15). Now, in the 21st century, Scott Williams is bringing us back to a biblical understanding of multi-ethnicity. In his challenging book Church Diversity: Sunday the Most Segregated Day of the Week, *Scott will lead you on a journey resulting in personal and church-wide awareness and growth.*

— Dr. Samuel R. Chand
Author of *Cracking Your Church's Culture Code*

Diversity doesn't happen by accident. For every cultural rainbow, both corporately and congregationally, you will find a leader who was intentional about diversity. This book will be confirmation for some and a push in the back for others, but it is necessary for all.

— Tim Ross
Tim Ross Ministries
(former Young Adult Pastor, The Potters House of Dallas)

Diversity is an urgent matter in today's global marketplace and in the economic conditions we face. Embracing diversity in the workplace and appealing to diverse customer groups is essential for survival and growth. Pastor Scott Williams challenges us to move beyond the workplace and create the same urgency in our house of worship, with a fundamental question: does the sign on your church's front door read EVERYONE WELCOME?

— Fields Jackson Jr.
Founder & CEO, *Racing Toward Diversity* Magazine

There is no greater challenge within the Church today than navigating the difficult waters of cultural differences within the congregation and within the community. However, there is no more important task than taking the gospel to every member of our community regardless of the cultural differences that may exist. Thus, the Church must confront this issue with tenacity to ensure we are truly reaching our Jerusalem, Judea, Samaria, and uttermost parts of the earth. Scott Williams brings us great truths and great insight on how church leaders can move beyond the errors of the past into a new era of Christ followers standing side by side, hand in hand, worshiping the King . . . regardless of ethnicity. This is God's plan and God's desire. Thank you, Scott, for helping us get there!

— Jonathan Falwell
Pastor, Thomas Road Baptist Church, Lynchburg, VA

An increasingly diverse society will not find credible the message of God's love for all people as proclaimed from segregated churches. In Church Diversity: Sunday, the Most Segregated Day of the Week, *Scott Williams provides a powerful, compelling, voice for a growing generation of church planters and pastors no longer interested in filling their pews with a homogeneous crowd but rather with the wonderful diversity of God's kingdom on earth as it is in heaven, all for the sake of the gospel.*

— Dr. Mark DeYmaz
Lead Pastor, Mosaic Church of Central Arkansas
Author of *Building a Healthy Multi-ethnic Church* and *Ethnic Blends*

Scott Williams delivers 100 percent straight talk in his new book, Church Diversity: Sunday the Most Segregated Day of the Week. *Pastor Williams calls out the elephant in the pew. With candor and passion he hits the bull's-eye with how ineffective the Church, at large, has been at closing the segregation gap. After providing historical context he unearths true stories of those that get diversity, do it, and how you can too. Christ prayed that we would all be one — this book brings us closer to being the answer to that prayer. A must-read for those who are determined to live centered in God's heart for His bride.*

— Tami Heim
Co-author *@stickyJesus: how to live out your faith online*
Partner, The A Group Brand Development, Brentwood, TN
Former President of Borders Inc.

What a remarkable and timely read on the extraordinary power of difference. Our generation needs a challenge far beyond the politically correct conversations on diversity. . . . And Scott delivers a tough, intentional yet hopeful one.

— Travis G. Mason
Public Policy team at Google

Acknowledgments

God: Thank You for placing the burden on my heart to see Your Church more unified. Thank You for giving me the platform to share this important message and a true passion for diversity. Thanks for Your definition of true love.

LaKendria: You are the love of my life and my best friend. Thanks for the encouragement, the nudge, the understanding, the patience, and the belief in me. I could not imagine this journey with anyone else on the planet. Our best days are yet to come.

Wesley and Jayden: Thanks for the kind words and the stories you contributed to the book. Thanks for being patient with daddy during his late nights and early mornings. Wesley, thanks for believing in me and calling me an author before I ever wrote a chapter. Jayden, thanks for saying, "Dad, when I get older I'm going to write a book just like you, except it's not going to take me as long."

Mom: Thanks for believing in me, even when I didn't always believe in myself. Thanks for challenging me to dream BIG and think BIGGER. You epitomize the notion that we tend to become what the most important people in our lives think we will become. I am better because of your undeniable belief in me.

Mari & Marc: Thanks for believing that your little brother could do BIG things.

My Team: N-Dub staff — We didn't just talk diversity, we believed it, we lived it, and together we experienced it. Thanks for believing in me. We Are Church Diversity!

Marvin: Thanks for taking the faith risk on me, by placing me in a major leadership role at a young age. Because you believed in me, I will always believe in others.

Pastor Craig: Thanks for your leadership and providing me the opportunity to live out my calling and be part of a truly amazing work of God.

The Pioneers: Honor and thanks to the sociologists, pastors, church planters, leaders, researchers, dreamers, authors, and others who have gone before me in this fight to see a little heaven on earth.

Liz: Thanks for believing in me and guiding me through the publishing process.

New Leaf Publishing Group team: Thanks for your hard work and belief in this project and allowing me the opportunity to share this important message with the world. I have appreciated your genuine commitment to your mission "To Bring the Lost to Christ and Balance to the Body of Christ."

My Friends and Family: Thanks for uploading your picture, for blogging about this book, tweeting about it, posting it to Facebook, providing input, making suggestions, challenging me, telling your friends, encouraging your pastor, sharing the message, praying, and believing that the Church can do better.

Behind the Scenes: Anyone that helped with anything on this project . . . you know who you are, thanks so much for your belief and commitment.

Contents

Foreword

Nine years ago I sat across the table from Scott Williams at a sandwich shop enjoying our first lunch together. At the time, Scott was working in corporate America and I served as a pastor. Although we had totally different backgrounds and skin color, we both loved and served Christ.

Scott explained to me that even though our church, LifeChurch.tv, was full of mostly white people, his African American family felt very loved by our church and called to it.

Two things became obvious to me before I had finished the first half of my turkey sandwich. First, Scott was a gifted leader. Second, Scott cared more about diversity in the church than anyone that I'd ever met.

Sensing a double opportunity, I bombarded Scott with questions. The first round of questions revolved around leadership issues, the second around diversity — especially within the Church.

No matter what I asked, Scott responded with a theory, a quote, or a strong, unbending opinion. After a full hour of lively discussion, I asked one final question that stumped him. Never short for words, Scott froze when I blindsided him with a question that would eventually impact us both in a significant way. "When are you going to join our staff at LifeChurch.tv," I asked, "and help us reach a broader audience for Christ?" I think I shocked myself as much as I did Scott.

Normally eloquent, Scott struggled to put together a coherent sentence. Although he couldn't answer my assertive question that day, several years later, Scott walked away from his upward track in politics, consulting, and entrepreneurial ventures to join our team as a campus pastor. From day one of Scott's ministry in our church, one of his biggest contributions to our team centered around helping to broaden the church's reach.

Five years later, after playing a major role in starting and building one of our strongest LifeChurch.tv campuses, it became obvious that Scott's ministry and message needed to go beyond the walls of our church. With my blessing, Scott decided to put more effort into getting the crucial message of diversity out into local churches across the world. The book you are holding is a significant part of his effort.

Chances are good that it is no accident you picked up this book. Just as God used Scott to help our church become more diverse, it's likely God wants to do the same for you.

As a white guy raised around mostly white people, I couldn't understand why a person of a different race or from a different background might feel unwelcome or disconnected by what we did in church. I also never realized that doing a few small things could make a big difference in who we could reach with the gospel of Christ. Although you may not agree with all of Scott's ideas, I promise you that he will push you, stretch you, and challenge you. Not only will *Church Diversity* enlarge your heart, but Scott will also show you practical ways to expand the reach of your ministry like he did for us. Most importantly, he will convince you that diversity is obtainable and move you to take a necessary step in the right direction.

As the diversity of our culture continues to increase, Christ's Church has not been keeping pace in many parts of the world. If I can be so bold to speak on behalf of God, I truly believe He wants this to change. The most diverse place in the world will be heaven. It's time for a little heaven on earth.

— Craig Groeschel
Senior Pastor, LifeChurch.tv

Introduction

I remember it as though it was yesterday; it was a cool Saturday evening in the fall of 2007. We had just finished our Saturday evening church services, and my family and I had decided to grab some dinner from one of our favorite restaurants — Chili's. We enjoy Chili's because of the consistency. You always know what you're going to get. At the time, my youngest son Jayden was four years old and my oldest son Wesley was eight. Dinner at restaurants is always fun with two little boys with BIG ol' personalities.

As we were finishing dinner, Jayden stated that he needed to use the restroom. Actually, Jayden loudly announced to us (and to the tables around us) that he needed to "do a *number FOUR.*" I'm thinking to myself, *I don't even want to ask what a number 4 is. That is a new one for me.* My sweet wife, LaKendria, leaned over and asked Jayden what a number 4 was. Jayden's extremely loud and bold response was: "Number 4 is diarrhea!" The entire restaurant was laughing. Those attention-grabbing happy birthday chants that restaurant servers do didn't have anything on my son. Jayden had everyone in the restaurant within earshot cracking up. We couldn't do anything but laugh; it was an entertaining moment to say the least.

Not only was Jayden entertaining, he provided a valuable lesson. Many times as leaders, pastors, parents, congregants, and spouses we see situations as though only number ones and number twos are available. We can only do things this way or that way — either black or white. The reality is there are many more variations of what we may have originally seen as only a number one or a number two. I often hear people say, "Well, that's the way we do this or that," or "It's our culture," or "We can't do this or that," or "It will never change, that's just how it is." We can't settle for "That's just the way it is," because we serve a God who is all about, "That's the way it *was*."

Assess → Believe → Change!

We have to learn to change our perspective, change the way we look at things. *If you change your perspective you change the game.* A perspective change will allow you to look for the number 4 option and not simply settle for the way things are. You begin to open your eyes and heart to what could be. You begin to look for that slight variation, because it might be just different enough to make a *big* difference. Some of the world's best success stories and most influential world changers are a result of their willingness to consider the "number 4" option. That's how LifeChurch.tv started video teaching: option number 1 (Craig live), option number 2 (someone other than Craig live), and option number 4 (show a recorded message of Craig). The rest is history, and multisite video teaching venues are popping up all around the world.

That's what this book is about. It's about "the Church" changing its perspective, which will ultimately change the game for the Church as we know it. This book is not about pointing fingers, but it is about speaking the truth and elevating the long overdue conversation of church diversity. The time is NOW and YOU are the change. Are you ready?

Assess → Believe → Change!

A Letter to God

Dear God,

Hey, it's me again! I wanted to write You a letter and share something that has been on my mind; actually it's been on my heart for quite some time. I'm telling You this as though You don't already know. Believe me, I understand that You're Mr. Omniscient and are more than aware of what's churning around inside of my little ol' head.

I've been troubled by this thing for as long as I can remember. "This thing" that I'm referring to is the fact that in the thousands of years that Your Church has been around, Your children just don't seem to get it. You're probably laughing out loud right now and softly saying, "Tell Me something I don't know." There are so many things that we don't understand, but the one thing in particular that has me all jacked up is the seemingly blatant unwillingness of Your children to worship together. You know, the whole — every tribe, every nation, and every tongue that the Bible talks about. Not to mention the Great Commission of making disciples of all nations.

Don't get me wrong, God; Your children do a great job of mixing it up with people of all races in many social and entertainment settings. They will even gather together to worship their favorite sports teams; however, getting together to worship You — not so much! The sad thing is that You probably don't even like most of the sports teams they worship anyway. If I had to guess, I'd probably say that You're a college football fan, think that we need to get rid of the BCS, and that You're ready for a playoff. Nonetheless, it's sad that we still haven't figured out how to get Your people to quit being so segregated on Sunday morning.

I know it must have put a big smile on Your face when, over 40 years ago, one of Your favorite sons — Dr. Martin Luther King Jr. — fought for racial equality in all areas, including the Church. Dr. King even said in one of his speeches, "We have to face the sad fact that on Sunday morning when we stand to sing, we stand in one of the most segregated hours in America." God, here we are over four decades later and not much has changed, and You know what? There are not many people who seem to really care.

I don't think that smile that Dr. King put on Your face has lasted for over 40 years; as a matter of fact, I bet You're frowning down on us right now. I know that we can do better and shouldn't settle for Your churches being these segregated institutions with parallel worlds that never seem to intersect. I don't have all of the answers; I actually have more questions than answers. I want to personally thank You for placing this burden of church diversity on my heart.

Again, I know You are probably frowning, and You are not alone. I frown with You. I know that we can do better, but I understand that change doesn't happen overnight. I do know this: we have to start somewhere and maybe that somewhere is right here, right now. Right here being the handoff of the over 40-year-old baton that Dr. King once carried. It's time for this generation of Your children to quit making excuses, to stop settling for comfort, and to cease blaming things on the generations before us. It's easy to make excuses and blame others. The burden for this generation is to look in the mirror, recognize that there is a problem, and understand that by doing nothing about it, WE ARE the problem.

Enough with my rambling, God. Let me go ahead and get to "The Ask." The ask is simply this: "God, please interrupt our lives. Disturb us. Challenge us. Make us dream BIG and think even BIGGER. Break us from the comfort of Church as we know it and help us to see Your Church on the colorful horizon of the future. God, please interrupt our visions of what is for visions of what can be. Let us not be satisfied with normal thoughts — move us into a place of abnormal thinking. God, please interrupt us and make the lack of church diversity an issue for all of us. Make our heart ache for the things that make You frown.

Sincerely,

Scott

1 The Most Segregated Day of the Week

The church that marries the spirit of an age becomes a widow in the next generation.

— Dean William Inge

Check out video 1
www.nlpg.com/churchdiversity

If you have read or glanced through the foreword and introduction and landed at the beginning of this chapter, I surmise that a few things may be true about you. You're standing in your local bookstore and find yourself curiously drawn to this red book with some dots on it titled *Church Diversity*. Although it's simple, the subtitle, *Sunday — The Most Segregated Day of the Week*, is a brutally honest and gut-wrenching reality. Some of you are skimming through the pages of a friend's copy, while others of you received a copy from someone who said, "You need to read this!" Some of you saw the link online, in a Twitter stream, Facebook update, or some other social media outlet. Those of you who love technology downloaded it to your iPad, Kindle, Nook, or e-reader of choice. No matter what brought you here, you are now at the beginning of a book that will courageously confront the black-and-white–striped pleasantly plump elephant in the pew known as Church Diversity. According to my sons, Wesley and Jayden, pleasantly plump is the politically correct term for *fat*.

Thanks for taking the first step and grabbing this book. My prayer is that you didn't just simply grab a book but that you picked up a piece of a movement. I ask that you journey with me as we ponder and confront this unnecessarily awkward issue that has long been ignored. Put on your seatbelt and remember that there are two exits: the first is right here and another at any page that follows this one. Feel free to exit this journey anytime you please. My hope is that when you land at the end of chapter 8 you will become part of a culture-changing and world-changing movement. *Church Diversity is more than a book — it's a movement of God, pastors, ministry leaders, volunteers, congregants, and the community at large.* This book is a tool that will foster having the tough conversations and encourage making the decisions that will change the face and heart of the Church. It's a tool to begin the conversation and help the Body Of Christ and ministry leaders to *confront the elephant in the pew.*

Church diversity on the surface may not initially seem like a felt need for everyone. If we dig down deep below the surface and get to the root of the matter, we should understand that "reaching all people for Christ" must be a felt need for the Church, and it can be a beautiful reality. Church diversity is about challenging ourselves to move beyond "what is" to "what will be." I like what the Bible says in Proverbs 16:2, "All a person's ways seem pure to them, but motives are weighed by the Lord."

It's not about the words, stories, controversy, title, or subject matter of this book; it's about the motive. The motive is to truly honor God by developing a movement of people who are willing to do whatever it takes to have His will done on earth as it is in heaven. Every time a group of visionaries begins the process of pointing toward the future and what will be, they begin to smile the smiles of tomorrow, today. That's what we have the opportunity to do; we can begin smiling tomorrow's smiles today. Smile, laugh, and imagine "what will be" as you read the pages of this book.

Part One: Where Have We Been?

It wasn't long ago (September 2009) that I had the opportunity to speak at one of the most unprecedented conferences of our time. The Nines Conference was facilitated by two of America's largest organizations for ministry leaders: Catalyst and Leadership Network. It was the first-ever completely online church conference featuring some of the world's top ministry leaders. Each leader was posed with this question: *If you had just nine minutes to share with church leaders, what would you tell them?* I did not have to blink an eye before I knew what I was going to share — I was going to share what has been burning inside me for quite some time. My plans were to get on the rooftop and yell very loudly, "Church diversity s—ks!" I wasn't going to really get on the rooftop and yell; however, I was going to try to articulate what I think is one of the more clearly visible problems facing the local church — the lack of ethnic diversity. "Church diversity s—s" may offend some of you; however, that was the actual title of my talk. For those who are offended by the title, let me ask you this question: are you offended because this pastor/author used the word "s—ks" or are you instead offended at the harsh reality that church diversity really does s—k in today's world? No one wants to touch this issue with a ten-foot pole, but that was before "we" took the bold step of beginning the conversation. Not only are we going to begin open dialogue about this issue, but we will also outline solutions designed to make a long-lasting difference.

As I was preparing for my talk for the Nines Conference, I was reflecting on my past experiences, my personal journey in dealing with church diversity, some pertinent historical thoughts, and some local Oklahoma City history that in my opinion parallels the subject. In the 1960s, Oklahoma City was a community that did not welcome black people in their eating establishments and had signs that said No Blacks Allowed or White Only.

There was a group of common, everyday people just like you and me that began to challenge culture on the issues of race and ethnicity of that era. These people had a belief that all restaurants should welcome everyone, no matter the color of their skin. Not only did they believe it, but they also put their money and energy where their hearts and mouths were and they did something about it. These groups of individuals would meet on the lawn of the somewhat run-down, but still standing, Calvary Baptist Church in Oklahoma City, Oklahoma. These meetings were the kickoff and platform for what would become peaceful sit-ins at restaurants throughout Oklahoma City.

During this same period of time, Calvary Baptist Church was looking for a new senior pastor and began to interview a number of different candidates. They brought one candidate to interview who was born and raised in Atlanta, Georgia. Although this candidate was sharp and appeared to have potential, the search committee that met behind closed doors thought that this young seminary graduate was too young and inexperienced to be the senior pastor of Calvary Baptist Church. That young pastoral candidate was Martin Luther King Jr.

It is amazing how each and every decision impacts history. Today's decisions will impact tomorrow's realities. The decision for this group of individuals to have peaceful sit-ins in Oklahoma City restaurants would ultimately change the face and heart of Oklahoma City. Each and every restaurant eventually put a sign on the door that said Everyone Welcome. The group of individuals at Calvary Baptist Church that passed on the young seminary graduate obviously impacted their church's potential in a major way. Seriously, Calvary Baptist Church could have potentially had *the* Dr. Martin Luther King Jr. as their senior pastor. Potential unrealized is just potential.

Dr. King went on to have a platform and support yet to be realized by any other minority leader, including Colin Powell and President Obama. As a matter of fact, Dr. King might go down as the most influential leader of the last century — period. He became the voice of reason that challenged a nation to no longer settle for the status quo and challenged the existing culture to change. He challenged us to not only have a dream but to make our dreams a reality. He challenged the Church to truly be the Church. In many ways, Dr. King is still the little voice of reason that whispers in our ear and gives us those subtle little reminders when we begin to ask questions like, "Can I (or we) do better?"

One of the most profound statements that Dr. King made over 40 years ago that unfortunately still rings true today is this: "We must face the sad fact that at the eleven o' clock hour on Sunday morning when we stand to sing, we stand in the most segregated hour in America . . . and the most segregated school is Sunday school." Ouch! Punch me in the face with a brick! Every time I read that quote I cringe inside. I cringe because we are a nation that has come so far in regard to race relations and racial equality. We have a black president, but when it comes to God's house or "the Church" we are still missing the mark. That statement made in 1968 is still very real and very true today.

That statement can and will be true 40 years from today if we don't begin to make mental shifts that I prayerfully hope will result in a heart-shifting movement that will ultimately change the face of the Church. A new and different future begins with the turning of these pages, taking this journey, having these difficult conversations, and addressing this pertinent need.

We are the change. We are the change that impacts our little pockets of the globe that we call our community. God has not only allowed you to be a part of your community, but you have been given the responsibility to influence your little piece of the globe. In no way am I audaciously assuming that you will single-handedly change the world; however, I am bold enough to say that you and I can and will change our own little piece of the world. A little spark is all it takes. As a child, I remember being told that sparks can start fires. That statement could not be more true. That little spark inside of you to "do the right thing" will help to ignite a fire that will change the complexion of the Church. Remember, little sparks can start big fires.

Dr. King's change began in his little piece of the globe, and before all was said and done, he impacted not just an entire nation but also the entire world. It goes without saying that Jesus' ministry in Israel was to be the kickoff and the beginning point of what would later be the proclamation and sharing of the gospel to all the peoples of the earth. His journey began impacting His little piece of the globe, and the end result is a ministry that lives, breathes, and continues to change the world by the second. Small moments of impact over time result in BIG change. We are responsible for making those impactful moments. We are that change!

Pastor Bill Hybels, in his book *Courageous Leadership*, shares one of the most simple but powerful quotes as it relates to changing the world and the hope for the world. Hybels writes, "The local church is the hope of the world and its future rests primarily in the hand of its leaders."[1] Hybels' quote is quite profound and comes with a great deal of responsibility for each and every one of us.

We have all been empowered by God to leave our little piece of the world different than when we found it. There is a responsibility to change, to have tough conversations, to make tough decisions, and to move past the Nobel Peace Prize–winning platitudes of "hope" and "change." We cannot just talk about the change, but instead we must be the change. We must be the carriers and manufacturers of the dreams.

When Dr. King so eloquently shared his dreams in the famous "I Have a Dream" speech, he shared his dreams that "little black boys and black girls will be able to join hands with little white boys and white girls as sisters and brothers." We are still dreaming and that dream still has not come true for the Church. I don't mean to speak on behalf of God, but I believe that the lack of effort on our part to come together breaks His heart. It's time to *move beyond the dream*. It's time to move beyond the status quo —in both the way we think and the actions we take.

It's become the "new normal" for sporting events, concerts, and other arenas to be filled with worshiping fans of all races, holding hands, cheering, yelling, shouting, and worshiping together. Unfortunately, that is not the "new normal" in God's House — the local church. Don't get me wrong; I acknowledge the fact that there are pockets of churches around the country that have figured out what it means to embrace diversity instead of tolerating it, and we will take an in-depth look at some of those churches and hear some of the stories of those leaders in chapter 5. We will develop an understanding of how these small stories affect the BIG picture. Unfortunately, these churches and leaders are the slim exception and should be the wide rule. Instead of settling for a few success stories, let's make the heart of these slim exceptions pave the way for the future of the Church — a future that looks totally different than the current reality.

The Early Church

In the Book of Acts, the Bible provides a vivid illustration of the importance of diversity in the early church, as well as outlining the controversy it can bring. Jesus' last words (Acts 1:8) were all about diversity and multi-ethnicity. Jesus corrected the disciples' question about restoring the kingdom to Israel, instead reminding them of their responsibility of witnessing the gospel and that their witness was not just to Israel but the world. In Acts 1:8 Jesus said, "But you will receive power when the Holy Spirit comes on you; and you will be my witnesses in Jerusalem, and in all Judea and Samaria, and to the ends of the earth." This is the theme for all of Acts. The first day of the church was strategic when Jerusalem was crowded with multi-ethnicity. There were not only Jewish pilgrims but local residents and devout men from every nation under heaven (Acts 2:5–11). The first church-wide controversy and conflict was about church diversity and multi-ethnicity — the Jerusalem Council (Acts 15).

Let's take a look at Scripture at a time when Jesus had just been crucified, rose again, and then ascended to the heavens. Shortly after these events, believers began to meet, giving us a glimpse of what the early Church looked like. Follow along in Acts 2:42–47 as we look at the interactions of the early Church and the original Church culture of celebrating diversity. This Acts 2 church was the first church to truly have a sign on the door that read EVERYONE WELCOME!

> They devoted themselves to the apostles' teaching and to fellowship, to the breaking of bread and to prayer. *Everyone* was filled with awe at the many wonders and signs performed by the apostles. *All the believers were together* and had *everything in common.* They sold property and possessions to give to *anyone* who had need. Every day they continued to meet together in the temple courts. They broke bread in their homes and ate together with glad and sincere hearts, praising God and enjoying the favor of *all the people.* And the Lord added to their number *daily* those who were being saved (Acts 2:42–47, emphasis added).

This Scripture is lined with inclusive words and phrases, such as "everyone," "all the believers," "everything in common," "all the people," "anyone," and so forth. The early church was on to something, as all the believers were together and they had everything in common. The "everything" that they had in common was Jesus.

A lot has happened since the early days of the church as described in the Book of Acts; however, the heart behind this first-century Christian Church should be the same heart that beats in the local church today. The heartbeat of the Church today is in need of a pacemaker to get back in rhythm and to set the pace for generations to come.

Where Have I Been?

Now that we've gotten a small glimpse into the early Church during biblical times and during the Civil Rights movement, I think it's appropriate for me to share who I am and where I've been. Who is Scott Williams and what gives him the street-cred (i.e., credibility) to write on this subject? I happen to be an African American male who grew up in the small town of Claremore just outside of Tulsa, Oklahoma. I attended a small "black Baptist church" in Claremore during my childhood years. As I got older my church attendance was what I would categorize as loose attendance. Our connections to the local church were, for the most part, "on again, off again."

As a teenager I would often attend church with some of my white teenage friends at what would stereotypically be categorized as a traditional "white Baptist church." I actually made the decision to commit my life to Christ as a teenager while attending one of those white Baptist churches with some friends. From an early age I had these bi-polar experiences relating to the ethnic make-up of church congregations. I grew up being *somewhat* welcomed in the "white Baptist church" youth group and *very* welcomed at my traditional "black Baptist church." I'm not exactly sure why that was the case. I think this was primarily due to the fact that I was one of the few black kids in a seemingly all-white community.

I was a known commodity and not the norm in the eyes of many. What is the norm anyway? I had come to realize that my view was not the same as that of my peers, the community, or even other cities around me. Although I felt somewhat welcomed, my eyes provided a snapshot of the challenges facing a nation as it relates to true racial reconciliation. People are quick to tolerate diversity; however, they are not so quick to truly embrace it and celebrate it. Embrace diversity. Don't just tolerate it.

Thinking back to my childhood, I believe that I have always had this ability to play in both courts, the stereotypical black courts and the stereotypical white courts. I embraced diversity even though people in both courts didn't always embrace my Rodney King "can't we all just get along" nature. I would receive awkward looks and comments from members of the "white churches" that communicated, *Why are you here? You don't really belong here. Shouldn't you be worshiping on the other side of the tracks?*

On the other hand, my black friends would call me an Oreo (black on the outside, white on the inside) for attending white churches and associating with the white kids. There is a phrase that applies to this context: "Too white to be black and too black to be white." I definitely wouldn't categorize myself that way; however, some naive people might. If I was going to be classified as an Oreo, I at least better be a Double Stuf Oreo, because the Double Stuf Oreo was the new Oreo that changed the game for Oreos as we knew it. Since the Oreo with double stuff was introduced, Oreo cookies now have many different varieties: Original, Double Stuf, Golden Uh-Oh with Chocolate Creme, Milk Chocolate Covered, 100 Calorie Oreos, Golden Original, Soft Cakesters Peanut Butter Creme, Golden Mini, Cakesters, Fudgees Chocolate Fudge Filling, Milk Chocolate Covered Mint, Chocolate Mini To Go Pack, and my favorite of course, the Variety 12 Pack. These Oreo flavors are somewhat representative of the different flavors of the Church. We shouldn't focus on our flavorful differences; instead we should realize the combination of different flavors is what makes all things good — just as the fact that all God's children are uniquely made illustrates the beauty represented by every nation and every tongue.

Those Oreo comments are seared into my memory. As I type these pages I vividly remember the ignorance and the naivety of those days. I have always believed that we could all "just get along." Deep down inside I have always been that double-stuffed Oreo wanting to be the game changer for Oreo cookies as we know them.

Enough with the Oreo analogy. But that leads into my next area of life experience.

Change Your Perspective, Change the Game

If you're like me and you've read this far about the lack of church diversity, you're ready to get to the point and learn the fix. I ask that you continue to journey with me and allow me to provide some context from my perspective. I believe it will not only shine a light on the problem, it will outline solutions and initiate a movement, a movement of people who are willing to Move Beyond the Dream. Life is all about perspective, so let's get some perspective.

In the summer of 1990, this small-town Claremore boy moved to the Big City of Tulsa, Oklahoma. Tulsa was definitely different from what I was used to. I made more black friends in a month than I had my entire life. New friends, new experiences, and an altogether new world. Although I lived in Tulsa, for a while I made the 25-minute commute to Claremore so I could finish my senior year of high school with the students I had grown up with. Here again I had these bi-polar experiences of hanging with the "boys in the hood" in Tulsa and my friends in small-town Claremore, where I was one of six black students in a graduating class of about 300. I came to realize that the only difference between the two groups was their unique perspectives. It was their particular set of circumstances and situations that affected their outlook.

One person's perspective will lead him to call someone else an Oreo. Another perspective will lead a group to look at someone funny who walks into their church and doesn't look like them. Yet another perspective will lead a group of Baptist church leaders to say that a non-denominational seeker church is not a real church, or it will lead a group of Christians around the globe to settle for pews filled with the same hues. The great thing about perspective is that it's experiential and it can be changed. Change your perspective, change the game!

I remember sitting through one of our LifeChurch.tv Partnership Experiences (aka Membership Class) one evening in January 2010, and those attending the class were sharing what they loved about LifeChurch.tv. The responses that we get during these experiences are generally the same; however, this particular evening one of the guys said something different. He was a young newlywed whose wedding ceremony I had performed a few days prior to this event. He made this statement: "The thing I love about this campus is the diversity. I was raised in a 'Podunk' Oklahoma town where people were just ignorant. It was nothing but white people, and I was ignorant as well. I love the diversity that's at this church and the diversity on stage during the weekend. It's changed my perspective; it's changed the way I look at life, people, and God."

Again, perspective is experiential and it can be changed. *Change your perspective, change the game!*

Those College Days

When I graduated from high school in 1991, my mom gave me three options: (1) join the military, (2) go to work, or (3) go to college. Since going to college seemed to be the least difficult and most appealing of the three, I decided to go to college on an academic scholarship to the University of Central Oklahoma, in the Oklahoma City suburb of Edmond. When I first moved to Edmond, I couldn't stand it, and now I love it. It is amazing how time and experience change perspective. Hmm. That seems to be the theme of life: *Time and experience change perspective. Change your perspective, change the game!* Today you couldn't pay me to move from Edmond. Well, you COULD actually pay me, but you would just have to pay a lot. I sit in my office right now, typing these pages from the great suburb of Edmond.

As a young man living in the dorms I had a deep desire to do something great. By living in the dorms, I was afforded the opportunity to meet a lot of interesting people and had a wide range of roommates. I had one roommate who was a country boy from Ponca City, Oklahoma. He would do the nastiest thing: he dipped tobacco. And what was worse was his overall tobacco-dipping process. He would roll some toilet paper up and put it in the bottom of an empty 20-ounce soda pop bottle and spit his sloppy brown dip in it. I'm sorry, but walking around with a bottle of spit is just nasty. The following semester I had another roommate on the opposite end of the you've-gotta-be-kidding-me continuum. When I walked into my dorm room on the first day of the semester he said, "What's up, blood? Are you a Crip?" Say what? . . . "No sir, I'm a psychology major." The unique thing about being in the Bible Belt in Oklahoma is the fact that even gang members go to church. Go figure!

It was a crazy time in my life, as I found myself hanging out with, going to the homes, and visiting the churches of all these different people: churches in the rural parts of Oklahoma, where I got the "Boy, what are you doing here?" look; charismatic-running-down-the-aisles-with-streamers-falling-out churches; traditional black churches that my roommates attended; a big, rich "white church" (and I'm not describing the color of the paint on the building); and the list goes on and on. You name the type of church, and I bet you that I visited it.

I would ask myself the same question every time I walked through the doors of a new church: "Do I feel welcome here?" That's the same question people coming through your church's doors every single Sunday are asking. Over the years, I could never get a clear answer to that question. If the answer is generally no or kinda-sorta — therein lies a deeper problem. I was always convinced that there was a deeper question that needed to be addressed.

The Shoeshine Man

Our experiences today shape our lives tomorrow. As I was trying to formulate a plan for where God would have me and my future family attend church, I continued to ponder that deeper unanswered question. What questions did I, or God's people in general, need to be asking? The heart behind that deeper unanswered question would be revealed to me, and it would come from one of the most unlikely places. Where, you may ask? The Shoeshine Man.

At the time, I was going to a great Spirit-filled African American church, and I remember needing to get my shoes shined. I always felt like I needed to be really sharp and dressed to a T when I attended this particular church. One afternoon I stopped by the local full-service carwash, and just like I always did, I got my shoes shined while waiting for my car to be cleaned. It's amazing the wisdom that you can glean from the local old-school shoeshine man. This particular shoeshine man's name was "Slim." Slim was an elderly black man who stood about six foot four with a jerry curl. (In case you don't know what that is, it's like the hair you saw in the movie *Coming to America*, with drippy juice that will leave a stain on your wall if he rubbed against it.) Slim was very tall and very slender . . . go figure. I'm sure Slim was his nickname, but that was his official name to me and every other customer.

As Slim and I talked about life during the course of my shoeshine, we somehow got on the subject of church and religion. I explained to him my frustrations and experience as it relates to the Church. I told him that I was looking for a church home, one that I could truly settle down in and one day raise a family in. Slim began to tell me about his church, and many of his descriptions brought back memories of the things that I liked from my previous church experiences. There were always different things that seemed to connect me to God in the churches that I had previously attended. Once Slim finished describing his church, I began to get excited and thought to myself, *Wow, this sounds like a place for me!*

My next question to Slim was this: "Is it a white church or a black church?" No sooner than the words came out of my mouth, Slim responded with words that I will never forget. He said: "Young man, that is the stupidest question you can ever ask. It's not a black church, it's not a white church, it's God's church. It doesn't matter what you look like. That's what's wrong with the Church today. So-called Christians are so worried about whether all of the faces of the congregation match their own that they miss the part about making sure their hearts match up with the heart of Jesus."

Ouch! Punch me in the face with two bricks. Those words wrecked me, but they wrecked me in a good way and I hope that they wreck you. I pray that God will use the pages of this book and the context of your experiences to *change the face and heart of the church*. Just like Slim said, my hope is that the heart of the Church will be less worried about whether the faces of the congregation match their own or things are done the way they always have been, and instead are more focused on making sure their hearts match up with the heart of Jesus and the heart of the early church in the Book of Acts. Just as the groups of individuals that orchestrated the peaceful sit-ins in Oklahoma City restaurants during the Civil Rights movement had a desire for everyone to truly be welcomed in every restaurant. Due to small impactful moments and demonstrations, the signs in Oklahoma City restaurants were eventually changed to read Everyone Welcome.

In another chapter I'll talk more about the church that I eventually attended and whether or not it was the church Slim was referring to.

Slim's comment changed my perspective and the way I thought about many things. Here I was, the guy who had the luxury of experiencing life in both worlds by playing "lifeball" on both the black and the white courts — and I was still missing the mark. I wasn't doing anything with my perspective; I wasn't doing anything with my experience. I committed from that point to not only "talk about it" but also "be about it" and put my "change money" where my "action mouth" was. I was going to be the Oreo with double stuff. I was going to be part of game-changing movements.

Prison Politics and the Pulpit

Let me share a little more of my personal story and testimony. I have not always been a pastor, and I have not always been a part of these game-changing movements that I'm referring to. As a matter of fact, I spent 11 years, 44 days, and 8 hours of my adult life in the prison system. It was as crazy as you can imagine: 8 x 10 cell, razor wire, bad food, pent-up anger . . . PRISON. Relax. I was actually a warden in the prison system. Why does a brother always have to be in the prison system? Unfortunately, some people did not even make it to this sentence as they said to themselves, "I'm not reading a book from a convict." For everyone else, the curious nature of human beings propelled you to read on. Thanks for doing so.

My first opportunity to have a major impact in the areas of race and ethnicity came in my mid-twenties. I was hired as one of the youngest prison wardens in the country. Prison wardens in their twenties, thirties, or forties are hard to come by; however, I had a leader who took a risk on me and would not settle for the status quo. This new role provided me the opportunity to make strategic hires and implement systems that would bridge the dotted lines of racial equality and connectedness behind the razor wire and cinder block of prison walls. If you think the Church is segregated, you need to spend some time on a prison yard. But since I don't recommend doing what my inmate friends did to get behind the walls, you can try being a volunteer or simply take a tour. I promise your overall experience will be better than if you take the criminal route!

I made small impacts and small changes over a period of time that had big results on an entire inmate and staff community. We had inmates of all different races eating together, engaging in recreational activities together, and even attending religious services together. We had staff members from rural Oklahoma who had never had any interaction with anyone other than "country white-folk," as they would refer to themselves. The other end of the spectrum consisted of staff members who were a few years removed from living "la vida loca," otherwise known as living the crazy life in the hood, and wanted to go into correctional vocation to make a difference.

I could actually write an entire book about crazy, awkward stories of uncomfortable and even life-threatening interactions based on race behind prison walls. Although it wasn't easy, we were able to make a diverse group of staff members work hand in hand toward a common goal. As we began to have the awkward, difficult conversations about race and ethnicity, we made diversity an issue worth talking about, and the result was a correctional institution that was recognized nationally for teamwork and for providing exemplary care for its inmate population. I learned a tremendous amount about race relations behind cinder block and razor wire.

My second major splash that made an impact in the area of bridging the lines of race and ethnicity came in the arena of politics. For the record, my heart is not to share politics, nor to mix politics and the Church; my intent is only to share my experiences to provide perspective. Please read the next few pages with that in mind. As we talk about traditions in the Church and people settling for stereotypes and the status quo, politics is definitely in the same boat.

As a young black man I was supposed to be a Democrat and vote a Democratic party line, right? That's just what you do in today's society. But I decided to take all of my life experience and perspective and make a decision for myself based upon my beliefs and my values, whether they were good or bad, right or wrong. I wanted to make my own educated, calculated, and appropriately contextual decisions. After much thought, consideration, prayer, and research, I did the unthinkable and I changed my political party affiliation. I became a Republican, a "Black Republican." (Insert: boos, smiles, applause, and shock and awe thoughts.) Not only did I change my party affiliation, but I also committed to putting my money (heart) where my mouth (action) was.

I began to spread the word and challenge people to evaluate their beliefs, experiences, and perspectives differently. I had a mentor in this area who had changed his political party affiliation a few years prior. His name was Currie Ballard and he was well known and respected nationally as a voice for black people. Currie was a historian and a nationally known collector of African American artifacts. He won an Emmy for a documentary that he made on the life of Dr. Martin Luther King Jr. In other words, Currie had the street-cred to be a Black Republican without having the Oreo tag.

Currie and I began to meet with the local party leadership in Oklahoma about raising awareness and confronting the other pleasantly plump elephant in the political pews: the general lack of black people and minorities involved in the Republican Party. We began to meet, raise awareness, advocate, provide a visible minority presence, and educate the public. We worked hard year after year to encourage people to be independent thinkers and not settle for the status quo. Our willingness to address issues of race and politics provided an outlet for people to begin to change their perspective.

In 2000 President George W. Bush received 4 percent of the black vote in Oklahoma. After small pushes, meetings, and challenges at the highest levels of the political arena, a group of independent minority thinkers began to make changes. We partnered with Oklahoma Republican Party leaders to challenge the system as it was. We were all a part of challenging an entire state to change. Four years later, President George W. Bush went on to receive nearly 20 percent of the black vote in the 2004 election. This was the highest percentage of swing for any state, and national party leaders began to contact Oklahoma State Party Chairman Gary Jones to try and figure out Oklahoma's strategy. Gary's strategy was simple: "The Republican party has a history of embracing diversity that seems to have gotten lost over the years. I want our party to be inclusive, so we had to make sure that we got the right people at the table and began having the right conversations and implementing the right strategies."

New York, New York — Big City of Dreams

The same year President Bush had the huge swing in the number of black votes he received, I had the privilege of being nominated as one of the first black delegates to the Republican National Convention from the state of Oklahoma. The icing on the cake was that the convention was being held in New York City. The NYPD had a Fort Knox security plan in place for convention delegates and attendees. I remember being on the Oklahoma delegation tour bus and looking out the window while we were on our way to the venue. I wasn't surprised to find out that not everyone in the melting pot was happy to see us. Some of the signs protestors held up, along with some of the chants, gave me the impression that they had some problems with the Republican Party and President Bush's leadership. I can't even include here the things people held up and shared in the name of free speech and civil disobedience. Nonetheless we kept rolling and the wheels on the bus went 'round and 'round. This was a big deal moment and the seriousness was evident from the real deal NYPD police hats, AK-47s, and officers on horses. This was definitely one of those experiences that engaged all five of your senses.

Once we finally arrived, I recall walking through the doors of the Republican National Convention and sitting on the floor of Madison Square Garden thinking, *This is pretty cool and I'm not even here to see the Knicks play.* I was soaking up all of the nostalgia — everything from hearing Mayor Rudi Giuliani, gospel artist Donnie McClurkin, Vice President Cheney, and a host of others speakers that performed on the big stage. The place was electric when they introduced the Governator from the state of California. Arnold Schwarzenegger brought the energy that this event was looking for, and he brought the house down with this classic Terminatoresque phrase.

Moments like this one reminded me of the words of Rodney King — "Can't we all just get along?" — and the words of the shoeshine man (paraphrasing), "There is not a political party for black people or white people, but they are both God's party." It's not necessarily the political parties that are jacked up, but rather that man makes our political parties imperfect. If we look back at the drastic change in the number of black votes President Bush received, it's important to remember that it wasn't as if 16 percent of the people went and changed their political party, it simply meant that 16 percent of the people changed the way they thought and changed the way they voted.

The premise of "moving beyond the dream" isn't designed for your church to go from being 100 percent white, Hispanic, or Asian church to a diverse church playing an entirely different genre of worship music overnight. The heart behind this movement is for any church, no matter the ethnic make-up, to begin the process of changing the way they think. Changing your perspective is the critical factor. In order for the Republican Party to be effective at going into every voting precinct and sharing their good political news with everyone, it was critical for them to be intentional in their efforts to be more racially inclusive. The Republican Party made a decision to have the awkward conversation and address the "hanging chad" of an elephant in the voting booth. The Republican Party had a perspective problem, and national party leadership made a commitment to change the perspective of the voting populous. The end result was the Republican National Convention having more minority delegates in 2004 than in the history of the Republican Party. Personally, I believe the drastic change was due to many groups of independent thinkers challenging the status quo and inspiring people in Oklahoma and around the country to change the way they think.

Over time, small impact made big change. The Republican Party, which was stereotypically thought of as "the most segregated party," was openly making changes to intentionally change the overall party perspective. That's the goal of church diversity: challenging people to change the way they think and the way they look at God's church. It should be a crime for Sunday to continue to remain the most segregated day of the week. As a matter of fact, it's almost offensive that the most creative, living, breathing, chosen vessel of the gospel can't seem to see past the complacent rut of church segregation.

As a "Black Republican" activist, I was truly able to be a part of a movement that affected a small piece of our national history: more black Republicans, more minority Republicans, more minorities in Republican leadership, more minority cabinet positions at the White House, more independent thinkers, and more importantly, more people challenging the status quo. The ripple effects of that 2004 movement have resulted in the Republican Party having the first African American party chair in 2008, former Lt. Governor of Maryland Michael Steele. The Church has to have the same mindset that State Republican Party Chairman Gary Jones had for the state Republican Party: if we want our Church to be inclusive and truly reach all people for Christ, we must get the right people to the table, have the right conversations, pray the right prayers, and change the face of the Church.

My experiences in Republican politics didn't necessarily have the same impact on our nation as Dr. King did. It didn't even have the impact that I believe this book will have on our nation; nonetheless, it did have an impact on an entire nation. That impact provides a clear illustration of how a group of individuals focused and committed to doing the right thing can have the right impact. Everything we do in life will have some sort of impact. It's not important to simply have an impact, but rather to have the right impact. There is a different kind of impact that a batter has when he hits a foul ball, as compared to hitting a ball that's going, going, and gone deep into center-field for a home run! We are called to have the right kind of impact. We may hit some foul balls; however, if we keep our eyes on the ball, over time we will hit the sweet spot.

I believe the right impact includes embracing the reality that all races can and should worship together. We must fight for not settling for the status quo, especially as it relates to race and ethnicity. Not only do I believe that you shouldn't settle, but I believe that you should put your money where your mouth is. I'm putting my money where my mouth is as I write the pages of this book. You are going to be challenged to put your money where your mouth is as you read the pages of this book.

We have established that church diversity is definitely an area that needs to be addressed and should be a felt need for all Christians — but where do we go from here? If the Church wants to truly connect with a lost and broken world, it must change and stop being stuck on the past. Churches that remain stuck with the spirit that believes that diversity doesn't matter, diversity is not a big deal, and church diversity is a non-issue will be totally left behind. We have come so far from the time when people couldn't vote because of the color of their skin. We actually live in a day and age where arguably the best rapper is white, the best golfer is black, the NBA center with the most potential was Asian, and the quarterback for America's team, the Dallas Cowboys, is Hispanic. I mention all this in order to show that the world is evolving in a good way as it relates to the issues of diversity outside of the four walls of the Church; however, the Church is at a red light. The brilliant Dean Inge of St. Paul's, London, said it best when he said, "The church that marries the spirit of an age becomes a widow in the next generation." The Church is the Bride of Christ and she shouldn't be the widow to any of His people. The time is now and we are the people.

The chapters to come will provide practical insights from my experiences at LifeChurch.tv and experiences with some of the top ministry leaders in the country, including Craig Groeschel. We will also take a look at the organizational playbooks of diversity-leading corporations like Coca-Cola and J. W. Marriot. Today church diversity is just a dream, a figment of our imagination. Tomorrow we will begin to "move beyond the dream" and make it a practical reality.

CHURCH DIVERSITY CHALLENGE 1

What is your personal history as it relates to issues of race and ethnicity?

How have your experiences shaped your belief as it relates to diversity?

Are you willing to be a part of the solution to affect positive change?

Endnotes
1. Bill Hybels, *Courageous Leadership* (Grand Rapids, MI: Zondervan, 2009).

Confront the Elephant in the Pew

When there is an elephant in the room, acknowledge it.

— Scott Williams

Confront the brutal facts.

—Jim Collins[1]

Check out video 2
www.nlpg.com/churchdiversity

One of my favorite leadership books, a book that in my opinion should be in the repertoire of every leader, is Jim Collins's *Good to Great*. This book has many great principles and concepts for business and ministry leaders, some of which we will discuss here.[2] One of the key thoughts that Collins rolls out is this: "Confront the brutal facts." That's the intellectual version of the saying "Just keepin' it real" made popular by Jeromey Rome from Martin Lawrence's 1990s hit sitcom *Martin*. When we don't keep it real and avoid confronting the brutal facts, what we are inevitably doing is negatively affecting our situation.

Some of the key thoughts that Collins outlines in his concept of confronting the brutal facts are as follows:

- Confront the brutal facts of the current reality head-on and leaders will emerge from adversity even stronger.
- Start with an honest and diligent effort to determine the brutal facts of a situation. It is impossible to make good decisions without looking at the entire process with the lens of an honest confrontation of the brutal facts.
- Create a culture where people have a tremendous opportunity to be heard and ultimately, for the truth to be heard.
- Stockdale Paradox: The Stockdale Paradox is named after Admiral Jim Stockdale, who was a United States military officer held captive for eight years during the Vietnam War. Stockdale was tortured more than 20 times by his captors, and never had much reason to believe he would survive the prison camp and someday get to see his wife again. And yet, as Stockdale told Collins, he never lost faith during

his ordeal: "I never doubted not only that I would get out, but also that I would prevail in the end and turn the experience into the defining event of my life, which, in retrospect, I would not trade." This paradox is about retaining absolute faith that you can and will prevail in the end, regardless of the difficulties, *and* at the same time confront the most brutal facts of your current reality, whatever they might be.

• Get staff to confront brutal facts. Leadership does not begin just with vision. It begins with getting people to confront brutal facts and act on the implications.

Collins has packaged an old saying in a fresh and easy-to-understand fashion. What Collins is talking about is the old adage of addressing the "elephant in the room." "The elephant in the room" is an idiom for an obvious truth that is being ignored or going unaddressed. The term is often used to describe an issue that involves a social taboo, such as race, religion, sexual orientation, or even suicide. It is applicable when a subject is emotionally charged and the people who might have spoken up decide that it is probably best avoided.

The idiomatic expression also applies to an obvious problem or risk no one wants to discuss. I think a blind man can see that we are not addressing the fat elephant in the sanctuaries and auditoriums of churches around the globe. Ministry leaders are claiming they want to share the gospel with "all people," but their sanctuaries and their hearts are communicating that they want to share the gospel with those that look like them. Where this becomes a problem is that in the history of the Church, ministry leaders are still trying to ignore the fact that there is big, fat elephant sitting in their sanctuary.

The concept of the "elephant in the room" is based on the idea that an elephant in a room would be impossible to overlook; thus, people in the room who pretend the elephant is not there have made a deliberate decision to do so. They are choosing to concern themselves with tangential, small, irrelevant issues rather than deal with the looming big one. I mean, seriously — ministry leaders spend more time worrying about the color of their carpet, what the deacons are doing, or how they can be the next relevant multisite church than they do reaching "all people" with the gospel.

Herding Elephants

We could make a strong argument that we have come a very long way in the area of dealing with race and ethnicity. However, we are far from arriving. Race is just one of those things that people would prefer to ignore and would rather not talk about. The problem with that approach is the fact that ignoring the elephant is not going to make the elephant (insert elephant noise) get up and waddle out of the sanctuary. As a matter of fact, the elephant has been sitting around for so long that he's lazy and doesn't want to move. There are pockets of leaders and churches poking and prodding at the elephant, but not enough to get the attention of his elephant siblings around the world. Herding elephants is not an easy thing to do, and herding racial elephants is ten times as hard as herding any other. The first step in herding elephants is acknowledging that they exist. No one wants to be ignored — that includes the racial elephant. Acknowledgment is the first step to getting it out of the room. When there is an elephant in the room, acknowledge it.

From the perspective of both an attendee and a staff member, I have taken on the informal role of the racial elephant herder. In other words, I'm that guy who brings the diversity conversation to the attention of my supervisors, peers, and subordinates. The more you confront the real issues of race, the less awkward they become. Sometimes I feel like I'm beating a dead horse (to use another idiom); nonetheless, I keep forcing the RMRT (the Right Message at the Right Time). The key is timing, because if you force the conversation all day, every day, and do it at times that are not right, your elephant herding will begin to fall on deaf ears. People need to hear the right message at the right time. If you share the exact same message over and over and not at the right times, those listening may experience what LifeChurch.tv Directional Leadership Team member Sam Roberts refers to as "numbness of frequency." People will get numb to the frequency of your message and tune your frequency out like a bad AM radio station.

I remember when I was originally hired as the campus pastor of the NW Oklahoma City Campus of LifeChurch.tv. Just for a point of clarification, the term "campus pastor" has nothing to do with college, but rather a term we use to refer to our different locations. I was so excited about all of the possibilities of this new community, new location, new people, and new potential. I made a promise to God that I would do everything in my power to be intentional about creating a culture and campus that truly embraced diversity. I remember it as though it was yesterday. I got in my car and drove around the area, praying for all that God would do and praying for a church congregation, staff, and community that truly embraced diversity rather than merely tolerating it. I didn't experience that type of heart posture at other churches that I was previously a part of. That's not to be critical; it's just the brutal facts. I actually never heard the word diversity used unless I was a part of the conversation, and I was perfectly okay with being the one who initiated those conversations. I would often tell people that I felt that part of my calling at LifeChurch.tv was to be a part of elevating the diversity conversation.

As I drove around, I went through neighborhoods and communities within a five-mile radius of a new and soon-to-be vibrant refurbished Wal-Mart storefront that would soon become known as the NW Oklahoma City Campus of LifeChurch.tv, aka "The N-Dub." I found myself pondering how we could impact this unique community that was comprised of everything from wealthy people to a strip of Section 8 housing and low-income apartment complexes located on an infamous street called Lyrewood Lane. The local fire department referred to it as Firewood Lane. The local police department called it Homicide Lane, and the rest of the community referred to it as Lyrehood Lane. Now mind you, this section was nestled off by itself and the majority of the surrounding area did not look anything like it. Like I said, we had all classes and races in this area.

I began to meet with local community leaders, one being the principal of the Tulakes Elementary School that was located on Lyrewood Lane. This guy was the real deal. He was an African American man named Lee Rowland, and he happened to be a minister as well. Lee was as sharp as a tack and a great man of God. He also had his thumb on the pulse of this community and a heart to truly make a difference. I remember my first meeting with Lee. I made a simple statement and asked him a simple question. *Statement*: We want to make a difference in this community. *Question*: What can we do to make a difference? That statement and question combination still remain at the core of our campus's relationship with Tulakes and the Lyrewood community to this today — nearly five years later.

I believe that the most important opportunity for a new ministry in a local community is to identify the top 10 community stakeholders and begin to develop a relationship with them. Some of these stakeholders will generally include local school leaders, elected officials, neighborhood associations, business leaders, and other community leaders. Ministry leaders should go to these stakeholders and see how they can help and how they can serve. Before the doors of our church ever opened we had the keys to the city, if you will, and definitely had potential to have the keys to the schools in our area. People in the community were excited and so were we. When the doors opened, we kicked off with a bang and saw little snippets of potential to make some positive headway in creating a culture that embraces diversity. Over the months we worked hard to reach the community, and within the first year we began to leverage our relationships with the local schools to impact their students. We invited the community and put a sign on our door that truly read EVERYONE WELCOME.

We had evangelistic bring-in events that would draw from 600 to 900 students on a Wednesday. That's right — 600 to 900 students at a campus that may have been running a couple thousand at the time. Those numbers were not the norm, as 400-plus students was a common occurrence. The kicker is that our student ministry was, for all intents and purposes, racially split down the middle — 50 percent black and 50 percent white, give or take a few. To top it all off, we had students from Lyrewood Lane and other areas walking to church, while we had students getting dropped off in Hummers and S550 Mercedes. This, my friends, is what you call an eclectic group for a ministry that is used to ministering to white suburbanites.

Our youth pastors were enjoying the challenge and had pure hearts; however, they had to face the harsh realities of herding elephants and realizing that they were going to have a lot to learn. They were forced to ask themselves questions about their life stories and upbringing. My associate youth pastor, Anna Meadows, was a 19-year-old young lady who was anointed and gifted far beyond her years — oftentimes referred to as a young Beth Moore. Anna was home-schooled by some amazing parents. They were cool, relevant Christian homeschoolers. Anna had zero experience dealing with the Ray-Rays of the world (translation: boyz from the hood) and was heartbroken by the struggles these students from our community faced. It was disheartening for her that the pizza we served was the only evening meal that some of these kids would eat. Although her heart was pure, the realities of embracing this new paradigm would require some adjustment and learning. My other youth pastor was Tony Cobb, who had a huge personality and was the mastermind of throwing the big "bring-in" event to get the students through the doors. The challenge for Tony was that the only experience he had dealing with minority kids, according to him, was when he was a youth pastor at Fellowship of the Woodlands, which is a huge church similar to LifeChurch.tv, in the suburbs of Houston. The minority kids included NBA basketball coach Avery Johnson's kid, which is a little bit different demographic than most of the kids who were rolling through our doors. To top it off, Tony opened up about some of his family history and how his grandfather was the grand wizard in the Ku Klux Klan. Yes, the one that wears the upgraded dunce suit — he wore the red one. Our discussion wasn't about Tony being part of a racist heritage; the fact of the matter was that when you begin to herd elephants, your life story becomes part of the process. You begin to notice little things inside of you and others that you would never have thought of before or would just like to forget. You begin to have "aha moments" — race is a real issue and you don't exactly know what to do about it. Have you had those aha moments? If not, there is a good chance you are avoiding confronting the brutal facts.

Over the months it became evident that we had some work to do in blending this culture of students to get them to worship, hang, play, and pray together. Our youth pastors/leaders dug in and began to develop relationships with students, which ignited a heart and passion to reach this new community and new demographic of students. The challenges we faced were not with the students; for the most part the challenges came from the parents and the leaders. Some parents were uncomfortable dropping their students off at a place that — in their mind —looked like the scene from an inner-city street basketball movie. On the other hand, we had leaders who were used to working with the suburbanites and didn't know what to say or how to address certain students.

At the time we had only one minority leader who happened to be an East Indian guy named Alex, and the funny thing is that one of my youth pastors thought Alex was black! What? Not even close! Eventually my sister-in-law got involved and that brought the minority youth leader grand total to two. We began to put systems and processes in place to help with integration and behavioral issues, but we still had the awkward parent and leader elephant that we needed to address. Each week more and more questions, concerns, issues, and perceptions developed about the demographics of the student population at our campus. This was truly an anomaly for LifeChurch.tv. The perception of this issue had gotten elevated to our Central Leadership Team. I remember talking to my youth pastors and letting them know that I was going to attend their leader meeting, and we were going to confront the pleasantly plump elephant in the pew. Well, not in the pew but rather in the multicolor chairs. My youth pastors were looking forward to the discussion and thought it was a good idea. It just became one of those issues where no one knew what to say or what to do. Leaders were saying things that were offending other leaders, youth pastors were saying things that offended leaders, and everyone had the same core agenda — make a difference in the lives of the students. The question was, "How do we move from where we are to where we need to be?"

The day prior to the meeting I remember being on a conference call with my youth pastors and their LifeChurch.tv central team leader. We were talking about a game plan for how to address some of the parent, leader, and student issues that we were having. I informed the central team leader that I would be going to the meeting and confronting the awkward subject of race. This form of ministry is called "calling a spade a spade." No sooner did I finish sharing my strategy, intentions, and game plans than the central team leader said this, "We are not going to make this about race. You are not going to go in there and make this an issue of race." I'm thinking to myself, *Seriously, do you want to have this conversation?* My response was, "Yes, I am going to make this about race, because it is about race." There were definitely some uncomfortable verbal exchanges before the conversation ended. That's what happens when you confront the brutal facts.

The next day I received a phone call and apology from the central team leader. He simply said, "Man, you were right. I just didn't want to make this a race issue. I know you have experience dealing with these issues, so we will just learn from you." I appreciated his acknowledgment of the problem, and the reality is that his sentiment is how most people think. They don't want to make this about race. They would rather keep a sleeping elephant sleeping. The problem is, the race elephant isn't sleeping; he's awake and we are just ignoring him.

The day after this call, I went in and led the AA meeting. Not the "Hi, my name is Scott and I'm an alcoholic" meeting." I led the meeting I call "from Awkward to Amazing" with an amazing group of student leaders. We talked about race and some of them shared the fact that truthfully they were uncomfortable interacting with some of these students and really didn't know what to say or do. Yes! We were getting somewhere. The conversations were initially Awkward but ultimately turned out Amazing. When you confront the elephant in the pew you move from Awkward to Amazing, and you begin the process of "moving beyond the dream." To make a long story short, our youth ministry became known as the rare breed of youth ministry that was racially split down the middle, and it became a ministry where race is literally a non-issue. The only way race will ever become a non-issue is if you make race an issue. You must confront the elephant in the pew.

Keys to Success

As I look back at the success we had in our student ministry in the area of embracing diversity, it made me realize that there were a number of things we did right. I am certain there are some things we could have done better; however, the end result was a campus and a youth ministry that truly embraced diversity from top to bottom. I definitely bought in to what God was doing. As a matter of fact, what we were experiencing was a result of answered prayers and a vision that God had laid on my heart many years before. It was amazing to see this newfound passion for diversity and the understanding that it was the right thing to do among our youth pastors, youth leaders, students, and the schools these students attended. Everyone began to catch the vision and began to have an understanding that what was happening was special.

What was once perceived as a burden — "What do we do with this diverse group of students?" — turned into a mantra: "There is just a small percentage of student ministries in the country that are doing what we are doing." It's always rewarding to champion something or to go where no man or woman has gone before, so to speak. What we were doing was working, and we were all still learning and growing together. The one driving force at the core of this culture of embracing diversity was the genuine passion to reach "all people and all students for Jesus." We didn't have to go to some Third World country to reach the least of these or share the gospel with all people; God was sending pockets of all peoples to our doors in the form of mid-high and senior-high students. These students and their families desperately needed Jesus just like every one of us does. The key for us was that we were able to see past where we were to where we needed to be. God sent us this diverse group of 400 to 500 students weekly to prepare us for what it would look and feel like to lead a church with a diverse adult congregation.

We had to be very intentional about assessing our diversity health. It's almost as if we went through a process and series of checkups. I have thought through some of the checkup criteria that helped us to successfully lead a culture that embraces diversity. If you want to live a healthy life, you need to have regular checkups, right? If you want to have a healthy culture that embraces diversity, you must also go through a process of checkups.

It's Time for a Checkup

Seven-Point Checkup

Check your heart. We had to start by asking the right questions, the difficult ones that got to the issues of the heart. If the heart is not right, nothing else matters. We didn't ask these difficult questions only about our ministry and our volunteers — we asked these difficult questions of ourselves. We all laid our past, family past, history, life experiences, and prejudices out on the table. We asked questions like: If I'm being honest, what prejudices or preconceptions may be getting in the way of my heart embracing a culture of diversity? Where is the heart of my leadership on the diversity issue? Have we led our volunteers and attendees to have hearts that embrace diversity? Is diversity a value that we genuinely want to embrace or is this simply lip service? The list of questions, revelations, evaluations, and assessments went on and on. Although it was not our only focus, checking our diversity heart rate was part of our daily journey.

Check your head. As we worked through the difficult questions in the heart check, we then began to focus on exercising our mental muscle. We had to plan events differently, we had to look at our hiring practices differently, and we had to be intentional about issues of race and ethnicity. We celebrated diversity wins, and although diversity may not have been at the forefront of the value system of the overall church, it was definitely at the forefront of our team's value system. I know God can do anything that He wants to do. However, if your heart is not right and you don't have a strategy for diversity, it's not going to happen. Your strategy can be as simple as, "Love God and love all people." If you don't truly check your mental muscle as they relate to a strategy to "love all people" and not just the people that look like you and your congregation, it's not going to happen. It's a matter of the heart and the mind. You have to dream BIG and think BIGGER. Exercising your mental muscle is the action step to making your dreams a reality.

Be prayerful. Ask God to give you a burden for diversity in the church. Don't confuse a burden for diversity with a change in the specific vision that God has given your church. Pray for diversity in people who will come through the doors of your church. Pray for diversity in both volunteer and paid staff. I remember praying daily for God to send diversity in our worship team, volunteers, first-time attendees, etc. My prayer was, "God, please plant the diversity seeds, and I promise under my leadership they will get love, sun, and water. We will commit to helping them grow." God must be involved in this conversation. Ask your church to pray for a diverse group of people to come through the doors. A church can't pray and have a vision to reach all people and not have diversity as a value. If diversity isn't a point of prayer and a value of consideration, the church should just pray and have a vision for a church that reaches a group of people that look a particular way. In the business of reaching people for Christ, that's called a prejudice prayer and a prejudice vision. Expand your prayers and ask God to expand the territory you are reaching for Jesus.

Be intentional. There is no other way to address this checkpoint than to say that if you are not trying to be intentional and purposeful about the church diversity issue, it's a non-issue. Do I mean affirmative action and classic diversity stock images in all media materials? You can call it what you want to and do it how you want to — the bottom line is if you are not intentional, it's not going to happen. Forced busing was intentional; mandatory interviewing of African American candidates for NFL head coaching jobs was intentional; and I can name ten other things that were intentional in forcing the issue of diversity. The reason you have to be intentional is that, left on our own, human beings often have difficulty making the right decisions. We were intentional about everything, so much so that I became known as the "Diversity Guy" and we were known as the "Diversity Campus."

Intentionality is about being deliberate with the actions that come as a result of exercising your mental muscle. Once, I was on a conference call in which all of the Oklahoma City Metro LifeChurch.tv Campuses were planning for a citywide event. The event was called LifeStock and it was a mash-up of Woodstock minus the negativity, with a huge church gathering, party, worship, amusement park, and all-around community event. This event was not only for all of the campuses, but it was to have a community outreach feel as we peacefully invaded and took over a local amusement park for the day. In the conference call we were discussing who was going to be on stage during the evening worship. I mentioned that we needed to be intentional about the band members and on-stage speakers being diverse. Another person stated they were not going to be doing anything intentional and that basically "it is what it is." That's not good enough when you have diversity in musicians across campuses. We were fortunate that I had just re-hired Stephen Cole as the new worship leader at my campus. Stephen is an amazing African American worship leader/Christian recording artist who has the talent and personality to fill up the stage. The fact that Stephen was now available to lead at LifeStock was one little piece of diversity that fell in our lap and wasn't a result of intentionality on the part of the event planning. The bottom line was that if Stephen and I were removed from the stage we would inadvertently advertise this citywide event as an event for young white people. That was definitely not the heart of the event. Without intentionality, the heart of an event, meeting, organization, gathering, or church can get lost. Being intentional about diversity is not about convenience, it's about being deliberate. It's the modern-day forced busing for the Church.

Be confrontational. The conversation between that pastor and myself was pretty confrontational, but it was necessary. If we are all brothers and sisters in Christ, we have to be willing to have the tough conversations with each other. Just like Jim Collins discusses in *Good to Great*, you have to confront the brutal facts. You have to confront the elephant in the pew, in our communities, in our ministries, and in our hearts. You have to fight for what's right. Pick and choose your battles. The modern-day battle for Jews and Gentiles to join together in one body and one Church and experience the promise of Christ is a battle worth fighting for.

Be authentic. Authenticity is so important. I like to use the phrase "Do you! It's a statement, not a question." That's the phrase I've used for many years to describe the importance of "being yourself." Too often we go through life and try to imitate other people. On an issue as sensitive as diversity, it would be easy to try to imitate a ministry that does a great job with the church diversity issue.

You know what I'm talking about. You find out what other churches and other people are doing and you try to do the exact same thing. Beyond attempting to replicate some of the things those leaders or ministries do well, you try to become who they are. I'm not saying that you shouldn't acknowledge and learn from others' strengths. In chapter 5 we will look at some ministries that are actually doing this thing we call church diversity well, in an attempt to learn from their successes. What I'm simply saying here is that you need to "do you." In other words, find your own voice/identity instead of being an imitation.

When I was called into full-time vocational ministry at my home church LifeChurch.tv, I was immediately surrounded by a lot of gifted leaders with some serious "skilz." It would have been easy for me to gravitate toward their style, their ways of thinking, and their particular cultural elements. I could have easily lost my own identity and originality. I had to recognize the tension of who I was created to be and what God has called me to do, while at the same time embracing the culture, DNA, values, and mores of the organization. If handled correctly, that's an appropriate tension to have. That same tension is important for the Church, as well. Make these heart changes and mental muscle changes, at the same time embracing the uniqueness of the vision for your church, ultimately understanding that the vision for the Church can't be outside of the important principles of what it means to be a Christian — love God, love your neighbor, and make disciples of all nations. Be authentic.

Be patient. It doesn't matter if you are a ministry leader wanting to create a culture that embraces diversity, a denominational leader wanting to do a diversity heart transplant for a conglomerate of churches, a volunteer that wants to have a diverse group of people serving alongside you, or a congregant that wants to see your church reflect the heart of Jesus — a church where everyone is welcome — it is necessary for you to be patient. This is going to take some time. It's taken thousands of years for the Church to be one of the most segregated institutions on the planet and change is not going to happen overnight. Get your heart right, exercise your mental muscle, be prayerful, be intentional, be confrontational, be authentic, and be patient. God's timing is perfect.

What You See Is What You Get

When it comes to what the congregation of a church looks like, it's usually a direct reflection of what is represented on the platform. One of the many questions that people walking through the doors of a church, especially for the first time, are asking is this, "Is there anyone in this church that looks like me?" Another question is, "Do I see someone like me on the platform, pulpit, or stage?"

When it comes to embracing a culture of diversity, too many churches miss the mark for the simple reason they have a *homogeneous platform*. By homogeneous platform I'm talking about the church platform, stage, pulpit — or whatever you call it — where everyone leading, talking, singing, and preaching is the same race and for the most part looks the same. If you were to name a church by the representation of their platform, the names of most churches would be as follows: Church of the Middle-Aged Skinny V-Neck T-Shirt White Guys, Church of African American Suits with Fat Knot Ties, First Church of Old White Men, International Church of Men in Robes, Calvary Church of White Hair, and so on. On a homogeneous platform, everyone you see on the stage looks the same from the perspective of race, ethnicity, and oftentimes style. People want to see themselves represented, and minorities will generally relate with another minority. If I am Hispanic or Asian I might feel welcome for the simple fact that I see an African American on stage or vice versa. There's something about being in a minority culture that makes you tend to relate to other minorities. I have heard similar stories from white people attending predominately black churches and immediately connecting with the few white minorities in those churches. The same thing is true for females; they are looking to see if they are represented in any shape, form, or fashion.

I remember a good friend of mine who attended a church where his was one of the small number of African American families that attended the church. He was bragging on the church to me and telling me how the church was impacting his life and family in general. After bragging and celebrating what was going on in his church, he said something to me that I will never forget. He said this: "Although we love what's going on at my church, it's challenging for me to bring my sons to a church where they never see anyone who looks like them in some sort of leadership role. I want to be able to point and say, 'Look — that could be you.' I want to give them something to aspire to. It may sound crazy or shallow, but it's real." I couldn't agree more; it's real. No matter the ethnic framework of your church, that simple truth is real, not only for my friend and his children, but it's true for people in general. I even heard my senior pastor Craig Groeschel mention something very similar when we had a world-renowned female speaker, advocate, and pastor from Hillsong Church — Christine Caine — speak at LifeChurch.tv. Craig mentioned that he wanted his daughters and other young ladies to be able to look up and say, "Hmm, that could be me one day."

Sometimes I hear people say that they don't really pay attention to the ethnic diversity or lack thereof on their stage or church platform. Generally speaking, individuals who say that are probably attending a church that does not have any reflection of ethnic diversity on their platform or in their congregation. Those churches that have ethnic diversity represented on their platform and in their congregation not only see it each and every week but they can feel it, love it, embrace it. It just feels good. A little glimpse of heaven. There is something distinct about a church culture that *at least considers* embracing the notion of every tribe and every tongue. A church doesn't want to be located on Sesame Street. "One of these things is not like the others. One of these things just doesn't belong. Can you tell which thing is not like the others, by the time we finish this worship song?"

Individuals who happen to be the ethnic minority of a particular church not only feel the presence of a diverse platform, but it speaks the love language of welcomeness not only to them but to everyone in the church. In other words, someone that looks like me — my cousin, my friend, my neighbor — is welcome here. That same love language of welcomeness translates to the ethnic majority of the church as well. There are many ways to begin the process of creating a culture of embracing diversity, and the first place to begin is having a diverse platform.

Theory of Looking-Glass Self

I remember back in my early days in college as a psychology major learning all of these really cool psychological theories and concepts. My knowledge and understanding of those concepts makes me smarter than you and allows me to have the supernatural ability to out-think you. As a college freshman, I think I really believed that to be true, but later found out — not so much. I did learn some cool theories. You have probably heard some of the theories: Pavlov's Salivating Dog Theory, Freud's Sexual Theories, Maslow's Hierarchy of Needs, and countless others.

One theory that always stood out in my head was Cooley's *Theory of Looking-Glass Self.* This theory is a social psychological concept created by Charles Horton Cooley in 1902. This theory basically states that a person's self grows out of society's interpersonal interactions and the perceptions of others. The term refers to the fact that people shape themselves based on other people's perceptions. As a result, people shape themselves based on what other people perceive, and confirm other people's opinions of themselves. They basically buy into the perception versus reality argument, and other people's perceptions become their reality.

The key concept of this theory as it relates to the Church and the importance of everyone seeing some representation of themselves in a leadership role is critical. Not being able to see a representation of themselves could create a barrier based on this looking-glass self theory. This is an important piece of information for the church to be cognizant of. This will help ensure that we truly place a high value on each and every individual walking through the doors of our churches. If the church is sensitive to this theory, leadership decisions will help individuals get over any mental barriers of perception and get to the place where they see themselves as God sees them. Whether we want to admit it or not, there is a perception versus reality tension that exists for people coming through the doors of the church — especially those walking through the doors for the first time. Embracing diversity will help people tear down any barriers to people beginning to see themselves as God sees them.

I remember having a conversation with a female pastor friend of mine about my buddy's thoughts regarding his sons being a part of a church where there are not any leaders that look like them. This female pastor attended the same church as my friend. She happens to be white and her husband is black. She said, "Wow. I didn't even notice these perception issues until my daughter said, 'Mom, why am I the only one that has a brown daddy that picks them up from class? Mom, why are none of my teachers brown like me and daddy?' " She didn't notice it, but her daughter did. Even though her daughter is growing up in the most colorblind generation of our time, she is still affected by this Looking-Glass Self Theory from a very early age.

This theory highlights the ways in which an individual's sense of self is derived from the perceptions of others. Just like the reflections in a mirror, the self depends on the perceived responses of others. According to Cooley, the looking-glass self is derived from three basic thoughts:

1. Envisioning how one appears to others. Asking questions like: I wonder what the people around me in church are thinking about the way I look. Do I fit in? Am I welcome? Can I connect with the God of the universe here?
2. Imagining what others must think of one's appearance. Since there are not many people that look like me, I bet the majority of the people don't even want me here.
3. Developing self-feeling — feelings such as pride. I am not going back to that church. I was definitely not comfortable or welcome, and remember, it's all about me and how I feel.

The Church can fall into the category of fostering environments that encourage these types of negative self-talk, instead of being intentional about breaking them down. Jesus created environments where no matter who you were you were truly welcomed and embraced in an awkwardly good way. Intentional love wins every time. If you are not intentional with your love, you can miss the mark. If you don't believe me, ask the countless married guys who think they are being loving husbands and because of the lack of intentionality, their wives don't even think they care about them.

"What you see is what you get" is all about intentionality. It's about breaking down the "Theory of Looking-Glass Self" to the "Theory of Christ in Me." The "Theory of Christ in Me" is when people begin to see themselves as Jesus sees them and they also begin to see the Christ that lives inside of them.

Is It Just about Race?

Every time I have a conversation about diversity in the Church with ministry leaders and congregants in general, the most commonly asked questions that I receive are (1) How do I incorporate diversity into my church? and (2) is church diversity only about race? Those are both great questions and I pray that concepts from this book will help to identify answers to the first question. The straightforward answer to the second question is, "No, church diversity isn't just about race." Ethnic diversity is a key component to the overall diversity conversation, because it's the one aspect of diversity that we can visually notice instantly. You can easily scan a sanctuary, lobby, Sunday school, or platform for ethnic diversity. It's much more difficult to scan for diversity in socioeconomics, age, interests, and background.

Imagine the person in the diagram on the next page is anywhere in a church and this is their visual spectrum being combined with their thought process. People subconsciously view their church experience through this spectrum. The conversation about race is where everything begins when you talk about diversity. As I mentioned, ethnic diversity is generally the one type of diversity that you can see and it's the most obvious. I can visually acknowledge that someone is Asian; however, I have a much harder time identifying whether or not someone is rich or poor. Socioeconomic status is a much more fluid type of diversity. It's one that you have to wonder about unless it's someone who comes to your church with the stereotypical homeless look, and even then there is no guarantee that's the case. The "homeless" look has actually evolved into a style of some sorts; as a matter of fact, many of you reading this have a band member or two that could stylistically fit the homeless build.

Again, the fact that ethnic diversity is the most obvious type of diversity provides a direct correlation to the other types of diversity. I see ethnic diversity and therefore I subconsciously assume that there is a mash-up of other diversity. Look at it from the perspective of this Diversity Spectrum Diagram.

1. I-See — you see some ethnic diversity.
2. I-Assume — you assume that other types of diversity exist.
3. I-Know — you look through the ethnic diversity spectrum out to the other layers: ethnic, socioeconomic, belief, sin, worship style, career type.

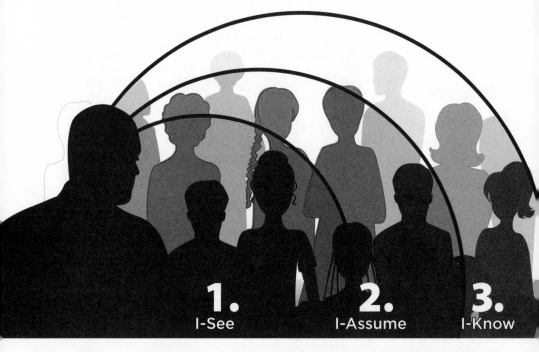

1.
I-See

2.
I-Assume

3.
I-Know

The Diversity Spectrum Diagram is important in understanding what lenses people are looking through as they walk through the doors of your church. What they see directly affects their perception of how they process their encounter with God, therefore directly affecting the Church's ability to reach the lost.

- **Does everyone in my church look like me**? If the answer is yes, I stop there and settle for "This is how it is" or "This is how it's supposed to be."
- **I see ethnic diversity within my church**. I begin to ask questions like, "Am I in the majority culture?" If I am in the majority culture, it's easy for me to spot individuals who are not in my culture. If I'm in the minority culture it's easy for me to not only spot individuals in the minority culture, but gravitate toward and have a desire to connect with them. I must be welcome here because they are welcome here.

- **I assume that other types of church diversity exist**. Because of the ethnic diversity that I see, I instinctively assume that other types of diversity exist. I begin to appreciate the spectrum of diversity that must exist within my church. Bring on the sinners in need of a Savior who don't look like me, talk like me, act like me, dress like me, and who have totally different backgrounds than me.
- **I see a sign on my church's door that reads Everyone Welcome**. I have reached the apex of how I view my church. My church is not just *talking* about reaching everyone for Christ — they are living it out. The sign on the door of my church reads Everyone Welcome.

Church diversity is not simply about the color of skin but rather people and the wages of sin. The wages of sin is death and there are people outside our church's doors who are going to hell. The Church must move beyond being concerned about "churchianity" or being the next relevant multisite movement to being more concerned about reaching all people for Christ. Church diversity is about reaching all people — period!

CHURCH DIVERSITY CHALLENGE 2

What does the "elephant in the pew" look like in your church?

What are some things keeping you from addressing the "elephant in the pew" and what steps do you need to take in your church to begin the process?

What challenges do you expect to encounter once you address the "elephant in the pew"? How are you prepared to handle these challenges?

If you were reading the sign on the front of your church, what would it say? If the sign wouldn't read Everyone Welcome, what can you and are you going to do to change it?

Share your thoughts on the diversity spectrum diagram. Are you able to move past I-See?

Endnotes

1. James C. Collins, *Good to Great: Why Some Companies Make the Leap — and Others Don't* (New York: HarperBusiness, 2001).
2. Ibid.

Everything Starts with Leadership: Leading Beyond the Dream

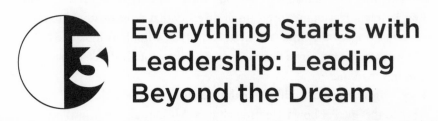

Leaders move people from where they are to where they need to be.

— Scott Williams

Check out video 3

www.nlpg.com/churchdiversity

The word "leadership," if taken seriously, comes with a great deal of responsibility. If you place the word "Christian" in front of the word leadership, you take leadership to a whole "nutha" level. When it comes to the subject of church diversity, most Christian leaders are absent. The term "absent" isn't used to be critical; it's just a reality that many Christian leaders will play it safe when it comes to this issue. Leaders are stuck in the chasm known as "comfortable familiarity" and therefore, make the issue of church diversity one of those "someone else's" backyard issues. The truth is it's not someone else's backyard, it's my backyard, your backyard, and the backyard of anyone who calls himself or herself a follower of Christ.

The time is now and the stakes are too high for us to just turn a blind eye and act like the problem doesn't exist or ignore the fact that this conversation needs to be elevated. Seriously, the United States has the first African American president in history and minority numbers are growing at a more rapid rate than ever in our history, especially in the Hispanic population. Due to the fact that culture and race are intersecting in so many areas, we are becoming a more racialized society. This is true for almost every entity except the Church. Racial lines are becoming more blurred than ever before. The Church can't afford to sit on the sidelines ignoring the coach's call to get in the game. We can't sit on the sidelines and ignore God's call for His Church. The Church is the hope of the world and the future primarily rests in the hands of its leaders. Those hands include the hands of every single one of you who is reading this book, those you influence, and those you interact with.

As we are talking about the future, let's take a look back to the past. I talked earlier about the shoeshine man named Slim who invited me to his church. Although I was intrigued, encouraged, and inspired by Slim's description of his church, I never attended. My church home selection came from one of the most unlikely places, the soccer field . . . call me Pele. My oldest son Wesley was in his very first season of soccer as a three year old around 2002. It was more comedy than soccer — we saw everything, including kids crying, playing in the dirt, picking up blades of grass, and kicking the ball the wrong way. We eventually put a stuffed purple dinosaur Barney in our goal and said something like, "Kick the ball to Barney."

During that inaugural soccer season, we met an amazing family who had a son that played on our team. We will just call them the Jossels — Keith and Charlesetta to be exact. They were a cool African American family with a passion for God, and their evangelistic spirit carried over to the soccer field. They invited my wife, LaKendria, and me to their church the entire season and we were definitely intrigued. We were familiar with their church and referred to it as "the church around the corner from our house that held up traffic." Seriously, this church used the county sheriff to direct traffic.

Charlesetta kindly informed us that the church was different than the churches we grew up being a part of. She informed us that the music was different, the dress was casual, the children's ministry was amazing, the teaching was biblically sound, the pastor was authentic, the teaching was applicable to life, and there were not many minority families. After an entire season of being invited, we decided to take the Jossels up on their offer.

That week seemed to pass by quickly as I anticipated experiencing church in a new — and what I thought was going to be very different — way. I remember getting ready that Sunday morning and asking my wife, "Do you think we can really dress down and if so, what exactly does that mean?" My dressing down ended up being slacks, dress shoes (freshly shined from my man Slim), and button-down, banded-collar Ralph Lauren polo shirt. Just typing that I wore a banded-collar shirt cracks me up. If you don't know what a banded-collar shirt is, imagine a Catholic priest's collared shirt. I was dressed to a T and I thought I was cooler than the other side of the pillow. But what might have been cool at my church wasn't so cool at this new drinking-coffee-in-the-sanctuary, super-casual, flip-flop–wearing church.

The building appeared to have a number of different entrances, and we really didn't know where to go or what to do. The easy solution if you don't know where to go is to follow the crowd, so that's what we did. I watched as people strolled in dressed very, very casual, thinking to myself, *I might need to untuck my shirt.* We made our way to the doors and let me tell you, we hit the jackpot because the children's check-in area was front and center. We received a warm welcome and we were excited to be able to check our son into the children's area. This was new, because children's church as we knew it consisted of scribbling and coloring on the offering envelopes, eating snacks, and playing around on the floor in between the pews. Once we checked our son into this amazing area for children, we made our way to the sanctuary, also known as the auditorium. We were greeted appropriately; however, we but were left to be anonymous for the most part.

The sanctuary was definitely different than what we were used to. It was dark and the room was filled with some smoky stuff and there was a rock concert playing on the stage. We went from listening to some Kirk Franklin gospel music in the car on the way to church to a full-blown Van Halen concert on stage. Seriously, one of the more stark differences was this rock 'n' roll praise and worship music. We sat down and listened to the message and we had barely gotten comfortable when the service was over. Are you kidding me, is this it? We just got here! We had just received some relevant biblical teaching, our son loved the place, and we were in and out in about an hour. I remember scanning the church to see if there was anyone that looked like us. By that I mean we did not see another black family in the place.

The entire next week we looked forward to attending our newfound church home, and each and every week, we ended up in its sanctuary and loved it. Our new church home was LifeChurch. The new hip name is LifeChurch.tv. No, it doesn't have a television studio; and, yes, there are now many of these .tv churches around the country. The more we fell in love with the church the more we realized that we had only seen a couple of other black families after several weeks of attending, and they were not the Jossels. My good friend Redell Brown and his wife, Nicole, were also attending, but they attended a different time than we did. For some reason, the fact that we didn't see anyone that looked like us speaking, greeting, leading, or serving didn't rest easy deep down inside. I found myself subconsciously thinking, *We like this place, but does this place really like us?* People didn't go out of their way to be friendly, but we were not sure if that was by design. I'm not even sure if that was true, but it was definitely my perception and perspective. We began asking the question, "Are we welcome here?"

Do the Right Thing Leadership

*That old law about "an eye for an eye"
leaves everybody blind. The time is always
right to do the right thing.*

— Martin Luther King Jr.

Each and every week that we attended I found myself wrestling with the gut-level question: "Is this a church where everyone is welcome?"

I had no reason to believe that everyone wasn't welcome; more importantly, I had no reason to believe that everyone was welcome. Many weeks into this internal debate a defining moment happened that totally changed the game for my family and me. A defining moment is one of those moments where you have a slight shift in perspective. Remember, if you change your perspective, you change the game. Senior Pastor Craig Groeschel was delivering his weekend sermon, and he came to a place where he read an e-mail from a church attendee. I can't recall the e-mail verbatim, but the gist of it was this: An African American lady had written about how she felt that she had been treated negatively because she was black and she was totally uncomfortable with her experience. Pastor Craig read the e-mail and then he took the entire congregation to the woodshed and verbally spanked them in a manner that I had never seen before from a senior pastor. Not only did he call attention to the e-mail, he clearly articulated that that's not the type of church they are, and if you think like this and treat people like this, this is not the church for you; you're a racist and you can leave now. . . . I'm not sure if it was exactly like that; however, that's how my mind remembers it.

I looked at my wife and said, "Wow!" I thought to myself, *Here is a really large church that only has a handful of black people or minorities, period, and we have just seen the senior pastor rail his 99.9 percent white congregation.* He could have easily tucked that e-mail into the DELETED folder. As a matter of fact, it did not even seem logical that his words would be beneficial to the congregation, but they were. Pastor Craig demonstrated the fundamental leadership principle that I call "Do the Right Thing Leadership." I remember people being extremely nice to my wife and me at the end of the service; this thick crowd of LifeChurch.tv attendees actually parted like the Red Sea. I think everyone thought my wife, LaKendria, was the one who had written the e-mail, or maybe it was because she was the only black woman in sight at the time. We were the odds-on favorite. It was on this day that people were overly friendly and Pastor Craig's words changed the perspective of the congregation that they definitely changed the perspective of this young black family looking for a church home to raise their children. We were down like four flat tires (translation: we were all in)!

I called the church offices not long after that to try to schedule a meeting with Pastor Craig. After sending a couple of e-mails as well, I received a follow-up e-mail that said that Craig had agreed to meet with me for lunch. His assistant scheduled the meeting for five or six weeks out, and I remember thinking, *I wonder why we are not meeting this afternoon. I guess this Pastor Craig guy is pretty busy.* Once it was time for our meeting, we met at Panera Bread. (Some things just don't get old and Panera is one of them. I like the frontega chicken sandwich minus the onions and a cup of broccoli and cheddar soup. That's a great sandwich and soup combo — can I get an "Amen"?)

It wasn't 10 or 15 minutes into our conversation after I thanked Craig for meeting with me and shared my story that I popped the question. No, I didn't propose, although I did propose a real question. I asked, "Pastor, where is your heart as it relates to diversity?"

He simply looked across the table and responded, "I have a heart for it. Will you help me?" Okay, now I'm down with this ministry like a car with four flat tires and no engine (translation: sign me up). These are the defining moments that change the course of a relationship and change the destination of a ministry. These are the moments where leaders move their people from where they are to where they need to be. Often leaders look for leadership principles to guide their decisions, and one of the best leadership principles at their disposal is the principle of "do the right thing." In my opinion, Pastor Craig exercised this principle when he boldly challenged his congregation. He unapologetically challenged them because it was the right thing to do. The same thing is true for the time when he looked across the table at lunch and asked me to help with church diversity. He did this first of all because his heart was genuinely in the right place and second, because it was the right thing to do. The road to Do the Right Thing Leadership sometimes begins with simply embracing the fact that you don't have all the answers and realizing that God brings people across our paths to help this "do the right thing" principle spread the name of Jesus.

American scholar Warren Bennis, who is widely regarded as a pioneer of the contemporary field of leadership studies, shares this perspective on Do the Right Thing Leadership: "Leaders are people who *do the right thing*; managers are people who do things right." The stakes are too high for Christian leaders to simply manage the safe expectations of denominations and culture. There should be no such thing as church business as usual. Do the Right Thing Leadership should be the banner that Christians proudly wave, similar to the heyday of the "What Would Jesus Do" bracelets. Jesus always did the right thing and it wasn't about the law or simply doing things a certain way. He just did the right thing.

Called to Do the Right Thing

I remember getting very excited early on about our newfound church home. It was evident LifeChurch.tv was led by a Do the Right Thing leader. I knew that I wanted to get more involved; however, I couldn't really articulate exactly what "more involved" actually meant. Was I "called" to be in full-time vocational ministry and leave my world of being a warden? (Why is it that we always think we have to work at the church instead of serve there?) Was I "called" to be a part of impacting this suburban ministry by being an active voice? Was I "called" to simply do the right thing?

Although I would have loved to leave the field of corrections and be on staff at LifeChurch.tv, that wasn't the right thing to do for that season in my life. God still had some more work to do in and through me before leading me into full-time vocational ministry. Instead of changing careers, we knew God had something different in store for us. So, for the next few years, my wife and I got plugged into volunteer service at LifeChurch.tv. And we loved it.

As I mentioned in chapter 1, I was able to be a part of some very special work of God behind the cinder blocks and razor wire of both adult and juvenile prison facilities. Our entire prison facility staff worked hard, played hard, and ultimately we were a part of changing the lives of the inmates. Additionally, I had previously been a political consultant, lobbyist, and political activist. Over the years, and through some amazing leadership opportunities as an entrepreneur, I interacted at some of the highest levels of our nation's political and correctional systems, and I had countless opportunities to act with moral and ethical integrity in what could be "sketchy" areas. I realized through all of my life experiences and education that God was preparing me for my calling; He was preparing me to do the right thing. Doing the right thing for me was taking that step into full-time vocational ministry in the church that my family and I had grown to love.

Upon being hired as a full-time pastor at LifeChurch.tv, there were some observations that became front and center realities. Sadly, they were like a mathematical equation:

No diversity on the staff + no diversity on the platform
= no diversity in the church

Not only was there minimal to no diversity in the people attending the church, the same thing was true for those who were on staff. There were just a few non-white staff members. And I mean just a few. Really, there were three of us! As a matter of fact, the guy who helped me along in my decision to do the right thing and take that plunge into full-time ministry at LifeChurch.tv was an African American man named John Davis. John was a senior leader at LifeChurch.tv, and during the time we spent together, I could tell that we had a kindred spirit as it related to diversity in the church and the impact that we could make as leaders on staff at a church like LifeChurch.tv. I also wasn't naive to the fact that LifeChurch.tv leadership specifically sent John to have conversations with me during my decision process. That is an important relational element to point out, because it holds true to the nature of this whole church diversity conversation and what it means to "lead beyond the dream." The reason John was asked to spend some time with me was because he and I could relate. He looked like me (kinda), and he talked like me (kinda), and in many ways he thought like me. John could convey that I would truly be embraced and welcomed as a part of the LifeChurch.tv team. That is the same confirmation that people who walk through the doors of our churches are looking for. Do I feel welcome here? Is there someone that I can relate to here? And ultimately, is everyone welcome here? Although there were only a few minorities on this staff of a couple hundred, I felt welcome. I don't know that I would have ever gotten to a place of peace in making this "do the right thing" decision if it weren't for John. John is one of the most brilliant, practical thinkers that I know. I always delight in the opportunities to argue, think, and strategize with John. The great thing is that even after five years on staff, John and I still regularly have these conversations about helping LifeChurch.tv and many other ministries to lead beyond the dream. We still have a lot of work to do.

Warden/Prison + Pastor/Church = Very Similar

There are definitely similarities between being a warden and being a pastor. I found that the most effective strategy for leading people is to "be about the people!" It's important to genuinely care and take care of inmates or church members. The method in which you lead people can cause them to either become a great asset or be a pain in the asset. Many times the inmates were my greatest assets as a leader, as they were the movers and shakers that got things done. They could make or break the success of our prison facility. The same is true for those who walk through the doors of our churches, as they can be the true carriers of the vision or the roadblock where the vision stops. In corrections and ministry, individuals are led by specific rules, identified culture, and organized structure. Like it or not, both places have clear sets of "do's" and "don'ts," and I would even argue that there are more do's and don'ts in the church than there are in the prison system. The church has way too many written and un-written rules: wear this or don't wear that, instrument or a cappella, sprinkle or submerge, this Bible version or that Bible version, tongues or no tongues, Internet church or physical church only, sloppy wet kiss (John Mark McMillan song "How He Loves Us"), or unforeseen kiss (David Crowder's version of McMillan's song), and the list goes on and on.

Additionally, inmates and church members act differently around the warden and the pastor. People in general talk and behave differently around pastors. In the same way, anytime I walked into a prison unit, all of the inmates and staff would be on their best behavior. Initially, inmates didn't want to be seen talking to the warden. Over time I gained enough credibility that it was no longer perceived as a negative thing or being a "snitch" if you were talking to the warden. Being a pastor takes acting differently to the next level. It's always fun to sit next to someone on an airplane and have a lengthy conversation with them before they pop "the question." Not long ago I was on a flight back from Miami, Florida, and got to sit by the sweetest lady. We talked and laughed throughout the flight. She was reading Chelsea Handler's book *Are You There, Vodka? It's Me, Chelsea*. She was telling me that the book is a bit tawdry; however, it's funny. She then asked me if I knew who Chelsea was and if I had read her books. I responded that I did know who she was but didn't read her books. Shortly after that she told me how much she travels for her job, and then she popped "the question." She asked me what I did for a living. When I told her I was a pastor the conversation immediately went south; she began repenting for reading the book and talking to me about looking for a new church. We talked the rest of the flight and I invited her to church. No matter where I go or what I do, people act differently when they know that I'm a pastor.

There are certainly similarities in the fact that prisons and churches are two of the most segregated institutions in America. This will remain true unless the issue is confronted. To this day you can find a prison yard in your state that is segregated, not forced but rather by choice. It's very similar to what you see in the movies: you have the blacks chillin' in this corner, the whites are over here, the Hispanics there, the Asians out there, and the sex offenders somewhat ostracized by everybody. The same thing is true for the church; for the most part churches are segregated institutions, and that segregation is by choice. Like it or not, the harsh reality is that both the prison and the church categorize and label sin. As far as sex offenders are concerned, let's be honest: sex offenders are definitely ostracized and not treated nicely in prison; they are considered the lowest of the low. If you put a truth serum in most Christians and church leaders they will tell you that they are uncomfortable around and even scared of sex offenders, especially when it comes to their children. Let's face it, insurance companies even have exclusionary clauses for churches that hire or allow sex offenders to volunteer; in other words, no coverage.

As a warden, dealing with issues of race, I did have the ability to force the integration and diversity conversation by inmate housing placement (what cellblock we placed them in) and having bold conversations with the staff and inmates. As a pastor, I can't force people of different ethnicities to come through the doors of my church; however, I can force the bold conversations with staff, volunteers, and congregants. Ultimately, a warden and a pastor lead a venue where people can be confronted, held accountable, developed, challenged, and leave personal chaos behind in order for their lives to be truly *changed!* Both leaders are called by God to do the right thing and to do as Jim Collins says, confront the brutal facts. The brutal facts are that as Christians we must be more concerned about spreading the gospel than we are about tradition and comfort. There is a reason that there was forced racial integration of schools, forced busing, and mandatory interviewing of minority candidates for NFL coaching positions. The brutal fact is that too often, if left on our own, we are sinful human beings and won't do anything about it. Ministry leaders, Christians, and those who care about doing the right thing: it's time to force the church diversity conversation and take the Church from where it is to where it needs to be.

As I was working on this chapter I was sitting in a little Asian-owned and operated coffee shop in my suburban hometown. There was an elderly white guy taking notes at the table across from me, two young guys who appeared to be part of a worship band because they were talking about their worship set for the weekend, and two college girls catty-corner from me talking about how much they loved Kanye West's music and how one of them just bought a glow-in-the-dark Kanye West T-shirt. There was a mash-up of race, culture, and entertainment going on around me. As I was multitasking/eavesdropping on all of the conversations around me, I received a phone call from a pastor friend of mine. His name is Artie Davis and he's a white guy who happens to be the senior pastor of the multiethnic church Cornerstone in rural South Carolina. I had the opportunity to share concepts from this book for the first time at The Sticks conference (a conference for ministry leaders in rural America) at Artie's church. Artie is passionate about diversity in the church and God was stirring in him. He had given me a call to get some things off of his chest. He told me how he took some of his African American staff members to a national church conference and the only black people in the room were the team members that he brought, and there was zero diversity represented among the speakers. We talked and brainstormed and strategized about what we could do, because we both believe deeply that this matters to the heart of God and that it's paramount to share the gospel with all people.

As I was on the phone with Artie, I received an instant message on Facebook from a guy by the name of Curtis. It is very normal for me to receive random messages, prayer requests, and questions via Facebook and Twitter. Although I'm friends with Curtis via Facebook, we had never had a conversation prior to this instant message. The message was brief and he was simply asking about why there is not any diversity represented at major church leadership confer-ences and a couple of other questions about diversity in mega churches. I paused for a minute, recognizing that there is no such thing as coincidences, but rather God choosing to remain anonymous. I then read the message to Artie and simply looked to heaven and said, "God, I'm listening. . . . Help me to share what Your people need to hear." I asked my new Facebook buddy Curtis to shoot me a direct message, telling him I'd respond to him later. Before I could get off the phone with Artie, I received the following message in my Facebook inbox:

> Hello Pastor Williams.
>
> I just IMd you a few minutes ago about black pastors and multira-cial congregations. It seems to me that I see a lot of white pastors with multiracial congregations, but when it comes to "minorities" pastoring the church we don't see the diversity there. I live in Washington right now and I don't know of any black pastors with a diverse congregation.

I know that we are all new creations in Christ and brothers and sisters in the Lord, but it is frustrating when you look at searches for the top Christian blogs/churches and you find no one from your racial background. I look at the major conferences and most of the speakers are always white with one or two minority speakers. Why is that? It's like in the business world where a company says they are diverse and when you look at management it's all white and the diversity comes at the non-management positions.

In the church I attend I'm one of, like, three brothers in there and from what I've seen, when brothers do come they hardly ever come back. The people are great at church but we don't do anything to attract the people that we are not seeing come to the church. Pastor believes that the Word is what will draw men and that we don't cater to any specific group of people. Anyhow thanks for your help . . . any pastors/ministries you can direct me to would be greatly appreciated.

Grace & peace,

Curtis

Curtis's words and questions were so timely. They speak to the fact that this is not just a white church issue, but rather a black, Asian, Hispanic, Indian . . . it's a capital "C" Church issue. Curtis is not the only one with these questions, although he may be one of the few that are bold enough to ask them. When you look in the mirror and ask the question, "Does church diversity matter when it comes to reaching all people for Christ?" the mirror should respond with a "yes."

A Holy Diatribe

I'm not sure if you are supposed to do this in a book, but I want to go on a bit of a rant. Let's take a look at the seemingly well-intentioned statement by Curtis's pastor: "Pastor believes that the Word is what will draw men and that we don't cater to any specific group of people." I agree that "the Word" is what men and women need; however, we are naive at best if we don't think that we have to do other things to draw people in. Those things are part of "the works" of ministry that God has called us to do. The statement of not catering to different groups of people is part of the problem and not part of the solution. As leaders we must cater to having a philosophy of "doing the right thing." The right thing as it relates to catering to specific groups simply means having a heart that embraces all groups, where the sign on the door reads EVERYONE WELCOME.

Leaders must begin to move and "lead beyond the dream," otherwise we will continue to have people like Curtis around the globe making statements like this: "In the church I attend I'm one of, like, three brothers in there and from what I've seen, when brothers do come they hardly ever come back." They don't come back because of the theory of looking-glass self — they don't see anyone that looks like them. They look through the spectrum and don't see themselves represented. The wording can be flipped any and every way. That statement happens to be Curtis's perspective. How about: "In the church I attend I'm one of, like, three Asians in there, and from what I've seen, when other Asians do come they hardly ever come back." This statement is true across the board, and as long as we take the common and comfortable position of Curtis's pastor and many others, we will continue to get the same results. Everything matters, even the little conversations, e-mails, thoughts, and decisions.

Little Things That Make a BIG Difference

Back in my days in the field of corrections and social services I remember having conversations about the national holidays that we observe. One of the companies that I worked for did not honor Martin Luther King Jr. Day (MLK Day) as an official company holiday. For some reason, certain organizations forget the BIG difference that it makes for organizations to honor MLK Day as one of their holidays. The *big* difference is not this overt — "Wow, look at the *big* difference" — but rather the little mental deposits that honoring the holiday makes in the hearts of the employees, their families, and the customers. In our case it was what it communicated to the staff, their families, and the inmates. I remember having several conversations with the CEO of our organization whose heart was already primed and ready to go as it relates to making the right BIG decisions. Because of his leadership, the organization quickly responded and made the right changes because "It's absolutely the right thing to do."

Once I began working at LifeChurch.tv, I remember having these déjà vu thoughts and déjà vu conversations about MLK Day: why in the world was it not one of the holidays that we honor? It was nowhere to be found on our official list of observed paid holidays. While we were at work on MLK Day, there was not a mention about the holiday even existing. For some reason, organizations don't want to make this adjustment because they are worrying about what doors it will open for other holidays and what people will think. The reality is that not honoring the holiday is more of a problem than honoring the holiday. It's the right thing to do — *period*! Each year as we approached MLK Day, I would have the conversation with our central team leader of human resources, Jerry Hurley, about the need for it to be one of the holidays that we honored. We would talk, he would listen, and nothing would happen. This was kind of odd to me, because in my opinion Jerry is one of the most logical thinkers that I know. He is the prime architect for the hiring of the LifeChurch.tv team. The problem with my "let's get 'er done" attitude is that I was thinking nothing was happening, but the reality was that I was making little deposits and little pushes on the flywheel. I was doing the little things that would ultimately make a BIG difference, and the bottom line is that I was doing the right thing. Sitting on the sidelines and not having the courage to say or do what's right is called being a coward. If you want to be a coward, hold your tongue; if you want to be a courageous "do the right thing" leader, simply "do the right thing."

After four years of having this conversation and Jerry telling me that he knew every year that I was going to give him a call, we began to make some progress. It's kind of crazy but the pendulum didn't finally swing on U.S. soil, it happened while we were on a trip to Ecuador. This was an amazing trip with all of the LifeChurch.tv campus pastors and several team leaders. We were sitting in the lobby of the Marriot Hotel in Quito, Ecuador, and having one of those RMRT (Right Message at the Right Time) conversations. Somehow we began to talk about MLK Day and how it needed to be a holiday that LifeChurch.tv observed. It was a great discussion and some of my campus pastor brethren were posing the argument against honoring it and how it wasn't necessary. It was one of those Pandora's Box conversations, as they thought that we would have to start honoring all of the other holidays. I continued to stick to my guns and make the consistent argument of why it matters, what it communicates, and that as the most innovative church in America, in my opinion we definitely needed to be on the right side of this conversation. At the end of the conversation, Jerry finally said, "We are going to do it, because at the end of the day the positive implications far outweigh any challenges. The reality is that it's just the right thing to do." Now, that's what I call a "do the right thing leader." Do the Right Thing leadership is an "over time" process and doesn't always happen instantaneously.

Unfortunately, we did not officially observe MLK Day this particular year; however, we had the right conversations and made progress. Martin Luther King Jr. began talking about Sunday being the most segregated day of the week as early as 1963 and there were plenty of accounts of him saying the same thing in the late 1960s. Here I am talking about the same thing over 40 years later. We are making progress. Sometimes you have to win over one person at a time, one conversation at a time. These conversations are never easy but always necessary. Little pushes on the flywheel help to spin up BIG change. If you are you looking for a way to start embracing diversity, make MLK Day an official holiday that your church or organization acknowledges. I'll talk more about MLK Day in the final chapter. Always stay focused on the issues and recognize that "getting there" takes time. Be consistent and deliberate while always keeping in mind: it's not about how you get from where you are to where you need to be; the objective is to get there.

Church Diversity Schools of Thought

Are you doing the right thing? Is your pastor doing the right thing? Is your favorite TV preacher or ministry leader doing the right thing? Let's start by defining what's right and what's real when it comes to church diversity. There are many different ideas, thoughts, and beliefs when it comes to addressing this subject, or any subject that involves race and ethnicity. I have identified three schools of thought that relate to understanding church diversity. Understanding the different schools of thought will help us get to a place where any ministry can begin to have success no matter where they are. In other words, these schools are great places to educate yourself on how you can be a part of a movement that moves your church and this discussion from where it is to where it needs to be. Remember, here is where you are and there is where you want to be.

The Schools of Church Diversity

The city. This is the most common school of thought. The philosophy behind this school of thought is simply this: the church should be a reflection of the demographics represented in the church's surrounding population. For instance, if the ethnic demographic make-up of a city is 75 percent white, 15 percent African American, 7 percent Hispanic, and 5 percent Asian, the church in that city should represent a similar demographic make-up. City demographics is a common school of thought in the church diversity conversation, as it seems to provide a holistic snapshot and starting place. This numeric barometer gives the local church a metric to strive for and a target to move toward. Again, this school of thought is a great starting place; however, it leads to a problem for those who are from the second school of thought.

The community. This school is the hardest nut to crack because there are generally deep cultural roots. The core belief of this school is: "Our church reflects our immediate local community." This school has a fair argument; however, it's not an excuse to settle for staying where you are. This school of thought must be intentional about reaching across community lines and exposing the leader and the congregants to groups that are not a part of "the community." The community school should engage in community swapping efforts, such as pulpit swaps with pastors outside of their community. The community school must be intentional about partnerships outside of the community. This school must take advantage of every opportunity to communicate to the church that "the community" does not supersede God's calling to reach all nations and Gentile inclusion.

The heart. This is the elite school of thought and the graduate school of the previous two. This school of thought simply believes that the heart of the leader and heart of the church will break down diversity barriers. If the church has a heart for diversity, people will drive many miles, across the train tracks and in and out of "the city" and "the community" to be a part of it. The basic tenant of "the heart" is based on the commandments of love. Not the lip service of love, but a true heart for diversity and a true heart for loving your neighbor as yourself. If your church truly has a heart for *loving* all people and embracing diversity, diversity will happen and you will get where you need to be.

What's Love Got to Do with It?

Pastor Rick Warren of Purpose Driven Connection explains the how, what, and why of love this way:

You show love by what you do, not just by what you feel. "Dear children, let us stop just saying we love each other; let us really show it by our actions" (1 John 3:18; NLT).

Love is more than attraction and more than arousal. It's also more than sentimentality, like so many of today's songs suggest. By this standard, is love dead when the emotion is gone? No, not at all. Because love is an action; love is a behavior. Over and over again, in the Bible, God commands us to love each other. And you can't command an emotion. If I told you right now, "Be sad!" you couldn't be sad on cue. Just like an actor, you can fake it, but we're not wired for our emotions to change on command. Have you ever told a little kid, "Be happy!" *I'm trying, daddy!*"

If love were just an emotion, then God couldn't command it. But love is something you do. It can produce emotion, but love is an action. The Bible says, "Let us stop just saying we love each other; let us really show it by our actions" (1 John 3:18; NLT). We can talk a good act: "I love people." But do we really love them? Do you really love them? Our love is revealed in how we act toward them.[1]

Love is a choice and a commitment. You *choose* to love or you *choose* not to love. Today we've bought into this myth that love is uncontrollable, that it's something that just happens to us and it's not something we control. In fact, even the language we use implies the uncontrollability of love. We say, "I *fell* in love," as if love is some kind of a ditch. It's like I'm walking along one day and *bam*! — I fall in love. I couldn't help myself. But I have to tell you the truth — that's not love. Love doesn't just happen to you. Love is a choice and it represents a commitment.

There's no doubt about it, that attraction is uncontrollable and arousal is uncontrollable. But attraction and arousal are not love. They can lead to love, but they are not love. Love is a choice.

You must choose to love God; he won't force you to love him (Deut. 30:20). You can thumb your nose at God and go a totally different way. You can destroy your life if you choose to do that. God still won't force you to love Him, because He knows love can't be forced. And this same principle is true about your relationships: you can choose to love others, but God won't force you to love anyone.[2]

The only way you get skilled at something is to practice. You do it over and over. The first time you do it, it feels awkward, but the more you do it, the better you become.

The same is true with love (1 John 4:7). Let's practice loving each other. As the Bible says, "Practice these things; be committed to them, so that your progress may be evident to all" (1 Tim. 4:15; HCS).[3]

My friend Pastor Rick eloquently outlined the reality of this love principle. The reason God's Church is not diverse is because His people have not learned to really love their neighbor as themselves. The Church must begin to practice the act over and over and over and over. If God's Church examines their heart and embraces "the Heart" school of thought, then progress will be evident to all and we will have more and more names of people written in the Book of Life.

Race and Culture

In their book *Breaking the Missional Code*,[4] authors Ed Stetzer and David Putnam talk about ethnic diversity and the ability to reach the unchurched. They write, "The growing number of unchurched people is just part of the story. The rest of the story is the growing diversity in North America. There was a day when a viable church in a community could be considered a major part of the solution. This is no longer true. Our growing cultural diversity requires a church within the reach of every people group, population segment, and cultural environment if we are to be faithful to the Great Commission." David goes on to write:

> I will never forget meeting with a group of second generation Koreans. Loyal by nature, they were greatly challenged by the need to plant the church among those who were born in a Korean family but raised in an American culture, speaking English as their primary language. Because of that dynamic, their language and experiences were radically different from that of their parents. In order for the gospel to be viable to their generation, they needed a church that spoke their cultural language. Breaking the code is about seeing the unchurched through three different sets of lenses that include people groups, population segments, and cultural environments. It is about seeing that our work as the church is not completed until God's kingdom has come home to every tribe within a given context.

Culturally Irrelevant

I remember the first time I drove by the church that sits right next door to my son's former elementary school in Edmond. The sign reads OKLAHOMA CITY CHINESE CHURCH; that definitely communicates that everyone is welcome. Well, at least everyone who is Chinese is welcome. I don't mean to knock this particular church, this was just a sign that I ran across. There are many of these cultural churches that place culture ahead of the gospel. They are spread throughout African American, Hispanic, Asian, and East Indian communities around the country and abroad.

I remember having a conversation with my children's pastor, who was a young, bright East Indian guy named Jayson John. (A couple of things that I learned about American East Indians from Jayson is that if they are Christians they generally have two first names and they are supposed to be doctors or engineers.) I learned a lot from him about his culture and the overall mindset of the cultural church in general. I interviewed Jayson about the cultural aspects of the "Indian" church. I truly believe Jayson's response speaks to the heart of this issue facing the cultural, ethnic, or first and second generation to American churches.

I want you to read Jayson's response through the lens of this super-bright 26-year-old Indian man married to a super-bright young doctor of physical therapy named Simi. They both love their family, culture, Jesus, and God's Word. Jayson has a heart for diversity and recently transitioned to being the director of community groups of a multicultural church in Oklahoma City (Peoples Church, featured in chapter 6). Jayson's response, in my opinion, is the heart and voice of what many believe but are not bold enough to say. He says:

> The issue of cultural relevance really hits home for me because I grew up in a church that was facing a cultural crisis. My parents immigrated to the United States from India over 30 years ago, and there was a fairly large south Indian diaspora living in America's heartland at the time. Naturally, since these people had similar backgrounds and spoke the same language, a community sprang up where they were living and at the center of this community was the church.
>
> Many of these people had young children, and their kids were now growing up in a culture that was so different from that of their parents. Over time, the church became a place where these immigrants could preserve their cultural background with all of its practices and traditions. They were probably shocked by some of the things they saw in America (remember they're just starting to see kissing in movies). You really can't blame them for wanting their kids to know about this part of their life. We, the second-generation Americans, were immersed in American culture everywhere we turned. It was integrated in what we learned at school, it was accommodated in every form of media to which we were exposed, and it was a huge part of most of the relationships we forged outside of church. In essence, the church was really the only place where we were exposed to the Indian culture.
>
> This became an issue over time as this second generation of Americans reached the age where we were growing more aware of this cultural disconnect. The leaders of the church had worked so hard to fight even the smallest infiltration of American culture into the church that soon young people were facing the reality that they lived in two

completely different worlds. By trying to remain relevant to their own cultural past, the leaders of this community had created a ministry environment that was completely irrelevant to the culture this new generation was living in.

The second generation was facing Western struggles each day, but their spiritual leadership was based on a purely Eastern approach. Dating is still considered taboo in India, but in America we were exposed to dating relationships in middle school, even elementary school in some instances. When I was growing up my friends were dating or talking to girls or starting to like girls or whatever else happens in the hormone-crazed minds of young boys. However, I had never, I repeat never, not in elementary school, not in middle school, not in high school, not even in college, and not when I graduated college, never heard someone teach about a biblical approach to relationships. Can you see how dangerous it could be for young people to grow up in a culture that is obsessed with this subject Monday through Friday, but go to a church on Sunday that doesn't even seem to exist in the same world?

Divorce is another cultural taboo in India. Though pastors are clear on what the Bible says, "God hates divorce," the same clarity is not given in conveying practical principles to be a better husband or better wife. I know of instances where pastors have offered no pre-marital counseling, but requested to see the bride's dress before the wedding so they can decide whether or not the dress is appropriate. I'm not saying that's wrong, but it's mind-boggling to think that the bride's dress is a more pressing concern than whether a couple has gone through counseling before their wedding.

You can't pretend that your church is immune from the culture that surrounds it. You can embrace the culture of your surroundings without compromising the foundations of your faith. This is absolutely necessary if you have any desire to win your community to Christ. The mandate of the church is to be a living organism outside its own walls. The great commission begins with "Go" not "Stay." The common thread between the Indian church I grew up in and many churches across the world today is that through an unwillingness to embrace and even engage culture we have essentially shut our doors to anyone who is different and have twisted Christ's command. We have confused holiness with elitism. We are called to be separate and set apart as holy unto the Lord, not because we are better than everyone else.

Most people would argue that I'm being unfair, and that culture is not as much a part of the foundation of the church as I'm making it out to be. It's difficult to understand until someone outside of your culture walks into your church. Does that person feel singled out? Does your church embrace people of other cultures or are they viewed as outsiders? They're not outside of grace, and they're not outside of Christ. They're not outside of God's love. They're outside of your culture, and if that has become the foundation of your church, your community is in trouble.

The Apostle Paul says it best: "For though I am free from all men, I have made myself a slave to all, so that I may win more. To the Jews I became as a Jew, so that I might win Jews; to those who are under the Law, as under the Law though not being myself under the Law, so that I might win those who are under the Law; to those who are without law, as without law, though not being without the law of God but under the law of Christ, so that I might win those who are without law. To the weak I became weak, that I might win the weak; I have become all things to all men, so that I may by all means save some" (1 Cor. 9:19–22; NASB).

Paul was not enslaved to any particular culture, but he was a bond-servant of Christ. Paul was willing to become all things to all people if it meant that he could save some. But this passage clearly shows that Paul was unwilling to compromise his beliefs. He became as one outside the law to those who were outside the law, but he was never outside the law of God. There are those matters where we as followers of Christ cannot bend or break. We really are called to be set apart, to be different. Paul understood this, but he wasn't driven by being set apart. When the ultimate goal becomes being different at some point we can become completely impossible to relate to. Paul knew it was important to be different. He wrote to the Romans that they must not be conformed to the patterns of the world, but Paul was driven by something else, and we see it in the next verse of 1 Corinthians chapter 9, verse 23: "I do all things for the sake of the gospel, so that I may become a fellow partaker of it." The reason Paul was a Jew to the Jews, and one under the law to those under the law, and outside the law to those outside the law, the reason Paul wanted to be all things to all people was for the sake of the gospel!

When I was a youth director, and still pretty young myself, I thought it would be great to offer something to the students at our church so they wouldn't feel left out of all the celebrations going on during Halloween. I knew there was no way the elders would let me do something on October 31, so I strategically planned for the cliché Fall Festival sometime in November. At the time our church didn't do much for our younger attendees outside of Sunday school, so I decided to go all out. We got tons of games and food and decorated our lobby. For the first time I can remember, people who didn't go to our church brought their kids and let them eat and play and be a part of our little community. It seemed like it was going to be a fantastic opportunity to introduce some people to the gospel. I made one killer mistake though. My lobby decorations included pumpkins. Next thing I know, people are yelling back and forth in the lobby and the parting words to me were, "You're corrupting the minds of our young people." Seriously! In a world of MTV and the Internet, pumpkins in the lobby are corrupting them?

Here is the point of my story. A church that had experienced little growth for years and years had an opportunity to be partakers in the gospel as Paul says, but the focus wasn't on the people who were there who needed Christ. The focus was on how we had brought aspects of American culture into our church. The church wasn't driven by the gospel. It was driven by preserving its culture. A church that is driven by the gospel is the living and active bride of Christ. It is a beacon of light to its community and it is a fortress of hope for the next generation. That church is relentless in its pursuit of those who are from Christ, and it is full of people who will say I will be all things to all people if it means saving some.

This is a wake-up call for the traditional ethnic churches, such as black, Indian, Asian, and Hispanic. The arguments that "we must remain separate because it's about the community" or "it's the only piece of culture that we have left" are not valid arguments. They are incongruent with who Jesus is and what the gospel is all about. Is your church about preserving the culture of some people or presenting the gospel to all people?

CHURCH DIVERSITY CHALLENGE 3

If a minority were to walk through the doors of your church today, how do you think he or she would feel?

Who is a leader that you admire for Doing the Right Thing? How have his or her "right thing" decisions impacted you?

What "Do the Right Thing" decisions have you made in your own church? How did these decisions impact your church?

What are some of the things keeping you from doing the right thing? How can you begin the process of removing these barriers?

Endnotes
1. http://profile.purposedriven.com/dailyhope/post.html?contentid=3330.
2. http://www.purposedriven.com/article.html?c=135708&l=1.
3. http://profile.purposedriven.com/dailyhope/post.html?contentid=3329.
4. Ed Stetzer and David Putman, *Breaking the Missional Code* (Nashville, TN: Broadman & Holman, 2006).

4 The Great Omission

They tell me that there is more integration in the entertaining world and other secular agencies than there is in the Christian church. How appalling that is.

— Dr. Martin Luther King Jr.[1]

Check out video 4
www.nlpg.com/churchdiversity

Do you remember the children's worship tune "Jesus Loves Me"? If you know the song, go ahead and sing it right now. (We will pause and wait for you to sing a few verses.) For those of you who don't remember it or have never heard it, it's this simple — "Jesus loves me, this I know, for the Bible tells me so." As Christians, we understand how we are supposed to live and interact with this world because of what the Bible tells us. The same thing is true for the Church. Most of what we know about the Church is because of what the Bible says and who Jesus is. Of course this is minus all of our man-inserted religious traditions. We are going to take a look at the church diversity conversation within the context of a scriptural WWJD, "What Would Jesus Do," and WWPS, "What Would Paul Say," perspective. Let me illustrate one thing that Paul did say as it relates to the unmitigated importance of church diversity: "This mystery is that through the gospel the Gentiles are heirs together with Israel, members together of one body, and sharers together in the promise in Christ Jesus" (Ephesians 3:6). We are called to be stewards of the mystery, understand the importance of Gentile inclusion, and embrace church diversity.

The Great Omission

Let's start with the basic premise of what Jesus tells us our mission is as the Body of Christ . In Matthew 28:16–20 Jesus was talking to His disciples when He said this: "Then the eleven disciples went to Galilee, to the mountain where Jesus had told them to go. When they saw him, they worshiped him; but some doubted. Then Jesus came to them and said, 'All authority in heaven and on earth has been given to me. Therefore go and make disciples of all nations, baptizing them in the name of the Father and of the Son and of the Holy Spirit, and teaching them to obey everything I have commanded you. And surely I am with you always, to the very end of the age.' " The imperative, "make disciples," first of all commits us to Jesus as Lord, Master, and Savior. This explains the central motive of the Great Commission, while the Greek principles translated "go, baptizing and teaching" describe the key aspects of what we are to do. *All nations* clearly articulates that Jesus' ministry in Israel was to be the kick-off and the beginning point of what would later be the proclamation of the gospel to all the peoples of the earth, people who look like you, me, those around the corner, across the tracks, and around the globe. All nations was about including not only Jews but also Gentiles. *Nations* is plural, referring to whites, blacks, Asians, Hispanics, Indians, and the list goes on and on. Jesus was clear about the Great Commission. More often than not, the Church wants to do what I have identified as the Great Omission. Churches start omitting the *all nations* part of the Great Commission and settle for simply making disciples and baptizing. Most churches take the arrogant and safe route of making disciples and baptizing people who look like them and their church. Why is it the Great Omission and not the Great Commission? Simply put, the church has dropped the *C*.

Jesus didn't call us to be safe and He definitely didn't call for us to be arrogant. The Great Commission is very simply stated yet vividly descriptive. Jesus didn't say you do this nation and the black people will do that nation and the Hispanic people will do that nation. The Great Commission tells us to have a heart for making disciples and baptizing all nations. Are you guilty of the great omission? Is your church guilty of the great omission? If we are being gut-level honest, the answer for most of us is an emphatic yes.

As many times as we have recited and read through that passage of Scripture, it seems as though the "all nations" part of the passage is simply a read-through that gets you to the end of the verse. Let's make disciples, baptize, and celebrate. Whoo-hoo! Slow down, reverse, and go back to interpreting the heart of what Jesus is saying. My interpretation is that Jesus is saying that as the Body of Christ, as represented in the local church, we need to be focused on making disciples of all people, all groups, all cities, and all lost people. He is telling us to get our hearts ready. It's one thing to give lip service and say that you are about all nations and loving all people. It's another thing to lie down on your pillow at night and wrestle with the heart of the matter. When it's only you and God wrestling around with what's inside your head and heart, the superficial lip service quickly subsides and reality takes center stage. You can't fool God, so go ahead and ask God to help you search your heart and soul on this issue. I will warn you to be careful, as often an exposed heart reveals the truth. Remember, as Christians it starts with the heart; let's begin by aligning our hearts with the heart of our Lord and Savior. Have a heart that embraces diversity.

Paul's Letter to the American Christians

Dr. Martin Luther King Jr. continues to surface in the pages of this book, primarily because he was so far ahead of his time in recognizing the need for God's people to have their hearts in proper alignment regarding the issues of equality, race, and ethnicity. He definitely drummed to a different beat, a beat that was in tune with God's drum.

Not only was Dr. King known for fighting for issues of equality, he was also known for many of his speeches, most notably his famous "I Have a Dream" speech. Our goal with *Church Diversity* the book and church diversity the movement is to "move beyond the dream." We want to move beyond where we are currently (Sunday, the most segregated day of the week), to where we need to be (a church where everyone is truly welcome). In order to move from where you are to where you need to be, we have to take a look at where Christians were in biblical times and where American Christians were in what I'm going to refer to as the "old days." If we take a look at the American Church in the mid-1950s and compare the Church to today, most people would assume that we have changed a lot. The reality is that the Church has definitely evolved, but one could also argue that the Church is still trapped in the pre-civil rights movement era. It was in this era that Dr. King not only fought for the advancement of civil rights, racial equality, and freedom; he fought for the advancement of the Church and Christians in general.

There is an amazingly rich and relevant letter that Dr. King wrote in 1956. I read this letter some years back and it wrecked me, as it forced me to take a look at the harsh reality of where the Church was from a global perspective and specifically where the Church was in the 1950s. This letter also struck a chord in my heart as I recognized the unfortunate analogy of where the Church was in the "old days" and where the Bride of Christ is in 2011.

Although Dr. King and others have tried to make strides and improvements, it's time to stop trying and start doing. In this chapter I want to share this letter in its entirety along with my thoughts and commentary. Dr. King wrote this fictional letter as if it were from the Apostle Paul to American Christians of the mid-20th century. It is loosely based on Paul's letter to the Romans. King turns up the heat as he urges his readers to deplore exploitative capitalism, spiritual arrogance, racial segregation, and self-righteous egotism, and he offers the remedy of Christian love. "Only through achieving this love," King writes, "can you expect to matriculate into the university of eternal life." As I stated in chapter 3, only through love will the Church matriculate to the graduate school of thought known as "the Heart."

I think it's important to feel the realities of Dr. King's day, his surroundings, the Church, the present, the past, and the future from the perspective of how the Apostle Paul might have shared it. Although this was titled "Paul's Letter to American Christians, November 4, 1956," it could very well have a title now that reads "Paul's Letter to American Christians, November 4, 2011." Or maybe even "The Scarlet Letter to the Church." Read this letter with an open mind and a heart that embraces the history and the struggle. Read this letter with a heart that understands the eerie correlation between the challenges with church diversity in the hearts of today's churches and today's Christians. Read this letter slowly, as though the words were flowing from the pen of the Apostle Paul with a kindred spirit to Dr. King. Feel the weight of his thoughts; allow his words to penetrate your heart. As Dr. King said, "Please read it as if you were reading it to your church, your pastor, your congregation, your family, your friends, and pass it along to other churches, pastors, and friends." Blog about it, tweet about it, post it to your Facebook page, share it at the next church or leadership conference, and put it on the front page of your website.[2]

Paul's Letter to American Christians, November 4, 1956, by Dr. Martin Luther King Jr.

I would like to share with you an imaginary letter from the pen of the Apostle Paul. The postmark reveals that it comes from the city of Ephesus. After opening the letter I discovered that it was written in Greek rather than English. At the top of the first page was this request: "Please read to your congregation as soon as possible, and then pass on to the other churches."

For several weeks I have worked assiduously with the translation. At times it has been difficult, but now I think I have deciphered its true meaning. May I hasten to say that if in presenting this letter the contents sound strangely Kingian instead of Paulinian, attribute it to my lack of complete objectivity rather than Paul's lack of clarity.

It is miraculous, indeed, that the Apostle Paul should be writing a letter to you and to me nearly 1,900 years after his last letter appeared in the New Testament. How this is possible is something of an enigma wrapped in mystery. The important thing, however, is that I can imagine the Apostle Paul writing a letter to American Christians in A.D. 1956. And here is the letter as it stands before me.

I, an apostle of Jesus Christ by the will of God, to you who are in America, grace be unto you, and peace from God our Father, through our Lord and Savior, Jesus Christ.

For many years I have longed to be able to come to see you. I have heard so much of you and of what you are doing. I have heard of the fascinating and astounding advances that you have made in the scientific realm. I have heard of your dashing subways and flashing airplanes. Through your scientific genius you have been able to dwarf distance and place time in chains. You have been able to carve highways through the stratosphere. So in your world you have made it possible to eat breakfast in New York City and dinner in Paris, France. I have also heard of your skyscraping buildings with their prodigious towers steeping heavenward. I have heard of your great medical advances, which have resulted in the curing of many dreaded plagues and diseases, and thereby prolonged your lives and made for greater security and physical well-being. All of that is marvelous. You can do so many things in your day that I could not do in the Greco-Roman world of my day. In your age you can travel distances in one day that took me three months to travel. That is wonderful. You have made tremendous strides in the areas of scientific and technological development.

But America, as I look at you from afar, I wonder whether your moral and spiritual progress has been commensurate with your scientific progress. It seems to me that your moral progress lags behind your scientific progress. Your poet Thoreau used to talk about "improved means to an unimproved end." How often this is true. You have allowed the material means by which you live to outdistance the spiritual ends for which you live. You have allowed your mentality to outrun your morality. You have allowed your civilization to outdistance your culture. Through your scientific genius you have made of the world a neighborhood, but through your moral and spiritual genius *you have failed to make of it a brotherhood.* So America, I would urge you to keep your moral advances abreast with your scientific advances.

It's amazing the scientific genius that has occurred. I mean, who would have thought that we would be able to read God's Word on our mobile devices? Millions and millions of people have downloaded the YouVersion Bible App and read billions of minutes of the Bible on their mobile devices. Many of you are actually reading this book in some sort of digital form. No matter what scientific genius we come up with, more than likely "there is an app for that." Unfortunately, there is not an app for the failed call of making Christianity a brotherhood for everyone and not just those who look like us. There's not an easy tap of the finger app for church diversity. Unfortunately, there's not an app for that . . . it requires intentionality.

I am impelled to write you concerning the responsibilities laid upon you to live as Christians in the midst of an unchristian world. That is what I had to do. That is what every Christian has to do. But I understand that there are many Christians in America who give their ultimate allegiance to man-made systems and customs. They are afraid to be different. Their great concern is to be accepted socially. They live by some such principle as this: "Everybody is doing it, so it must be alright." For so many of you Morality is merely group consensus. In your modern sociological lingo, the mores are accepted as the right ways. You have unconsciously come to believe that right is discovered by taking a sort of Gallup poll of the majority opinion. How many are giving their ultimate allegiance to this way.

But American Christians, I must say to you as I said to the Roman Christians years ago, "Be not conformed to this world, but be ye transformed by the renewing of your mind." Or, as I said to the Philippian Christians, "Ye are a colony of heaven." This means that although you live in the colony of time, your ultimate allegiance is to the empire of eternity. You have a dual citizenry. You live both in time and eternity; both in heaven and earth. Therefore, your ultimate allegiance is not to the government, not to the state, not to the nation, not to any man-made institution. The Christian owes his ultimate allegiance to God, and if any earthly institution conflicts with God's will, it is your Christian duty to take a stand against it. You must never allow the transitory evanescent demands of man-made institutions to take precedence over the eternal demands of the Almighty God.

Wow! This lays out the whole "God's will being done on earth as it is in heaven" standard. Just because every new, hot, contemporary, fast-growing, top-of-the-list church has middle-age white guys in skinny jeans doesn't mean that's the standard for your church. Some churches have settled for copycatting the things that really don't amount to a hill of beans. I'm not really sure what a hill of beans is, but I'm assuming that means it doesn't amount to anything. God, help us to move past the status quo demands of the manmade standards and rules for what the Church should look like. Help us to move toward Your painting of the Church and the mission that Jesus laid out for the Church.

> I understand that you have an economic system in America known as Capitalism. Through this economic system you have been able to do wonders. You have become the richest nation in the world, and you have built up the greatest system of production that history has ever known. All of this is marvelous. But, Americans, there is the danger that you will misuse your Capitalism. I still contend that money can be the root of all evil. It can cause one to live a life of gross materialism. I am afraid that many among you are more concerned about making a living than making a life. You are prone to judge the success of your profession by the index of your salary and the size of the wheelbase on your automobile, rather than the quality of your service to humanity.

The Church is quick to judge its success based on numerical growth with zero consideration for growth of the nations within the Church.

> The misuse of Capitalism can also lead to tragic exploitation. This has so often happened in your nation. They tell me that one-tenth of 1 percent of the population controls more than 40 percent of the wealth. Oh, America, how often have you taken necessities from the masses to give luxuries to the

classes. If you are to be a truly Christian nation, you must solve this problem. You cannot solve the problem by turning to communism, for communism is based on an ethical relativism and a metaphysical materialism that no Christian can accept. You can work within the framework of democracy to bring about a better distribution of wealth. You can use your powerful economic resources to wipe poverty from the face of the earth. God never intended for one group of people to live in superfluous inordinate wealth, while others live in abject deadening poverty. God intends for all of His children to have the basic necessities of life, and He has left in this universe "enough and to spare" for that purpose. So I call upon you to bridge the gulf between abject poverty and superfluous wealth.

I would that I could be with you in person, so that I could say to you face to face what I am forced to say to you in writing. Oh, how I long to share your fellowship.

Let me rush on to say something about the church. Americans, I must remind you, as I have said to so many others, that the church is the Body of Christ. *So when the church is true to its nature it knows neither division nor disunity.* But I am disturbed about what you are doing to the Body of Christ. *They tell me that in America you have within Protestantism more than two hundred and fifty-six denominations* [emphasis added]. The tragedy is not so much that you have such a multiplicity of denominations, but that most of them are warring against each other with a claim to absolute truth. This narrow sectarianism is destroying the unity of the Body of Christ. You must come to see that God is neither a Baptist nor a Methodist; He is neither a Presbyterian nor an Episcopalian. God is bigger than all of our denominations. If you are to be true witnesses for Christ, you must come to see that, America.

We care more about our denominational differences than we do the basic tenet of the first and greatest commandment — loving our neighbor as ourselves. God is bigger than any denomination. As we continue to tear down the walls of denominationalism, let us not forget the walls of racism. That is such a difficult word to digest, especially when it's tied to the Body of Christ. Let us not be naive. All too recently there have been many challenges with the Church and specific denominations embracing minorities by having them fill legitimate pastoral roles. According to the book *Race and the Assemblies of God Church*, "The Assemblies of God Church was known for a racist and late to embracing diversity party. The Assemblies of God Church was exploding with the attitude of every nation and every tongue overseas, while excluding certain ethnic groups from fellowship and worship. Social developments in the 1950s and 1960s initiated gradual changes in attitudes toward race in the Assemblies of God that ultimately resulted in the church's disavowal of its racist past in 1994. However, there is little evidence that the leadership's efforts to reconcile with the African American Pentecostal community has fostered any substantial efforts to do so among the churches in the denomination."[3] This isn't to be critical of the Assemblies of God Church, as many denominations have issues with race relations. I'm simply trying to promote awareness and acknowledgment of the fact that the issues of overt racism, the church, and academia date back to as recently as the 1990s. This same heart posture existed in educational circles, even at what is considered a premier seminary program, the Dallas Theological Seminary (DTS). It was just in 1982 that DTS awarded a doctorate to Tony Evans, the first African American to receive a ThD from that prestigious institution. That is not a typo, 1982. Seriously, that was not very many years ago.

Enough with the protestant church. Let's find out what the pen of the Apostle Paul has to say through the mind of Dr. King about the Catholic Church.

> But I must not stop with a criticism of Protestantism. I am disturbed about Roman Catholicism. This church stands before the world with its pomp and power, insisting that it possesses the only truth. It incorporates an arrogance that becomes a dangerous spiritual arrogance. It stands with its noble Pope who somehow rises to the miraculous heights of infallibility when he speaks ex cathedra. But I am disturbed about a person or an institution that claims infallibility in this world. I am disturbed about any church that refuses to cooperate with other churches under the pretense that it is the only true church. I must emphasize the fact that God is not a Roman Catholic, and that the boundless sweep of His revelation cannot be limited to the Vatican. Roman Catholicism must do a great deal to mend its ways.

Church diversity is not simply an issue isolated to a particular denomination; its lineage goes across denominational lines. There are even challenges with church diversity in the Roman Catholic Church that Dr. King refers to. The Catholic Church is publicly recognizing a need to make adjustments to how they view church diversity. In May of 2010, 300 church leaders — bishops, priests, religious, and laity — from all ethnic and cultural families and walks of life gathered at the University of Notre Dame for the Catholic Cultural Diversity Network Convocation (CCDNC). The gathering coincided with the tenth anniversary of Encuentro 2000, the Millennial Jubilee multicultural celebration. The purpose "was to continue the dialogue initiated a decade before, by highlighting the challenges and opportunities in linking the Church's growing racial, cultural, and ethnic diversity with the need to foster a robust Catholic identity."[4] The process responds to the priority of the United States Conference of Catholic Bishops (USCCB) on cultural diversity and is a first step in developing and widely disseminating intercultural competency guidelines. "It is no secret that most U.S. Catholic parishes, dioceses, schools, and organizations as well as the ranks of the clergy, religious, and lay leaders are undergoing a profound change as a result of dramatic demographic shifts," said Jesuit Father Allan F. Deck, executive director of the USCCB Secretariat of Cultural Diversity in the Church. This convocation provided leaders with an opportunity to share stories within their own communities and with a wider cross-section of colleagues from other communities. In my opinion, the Catholic Church wrestled with three questions that the Church as a whole needs to wrestle with:

1. How do today's diverse members of the Church understand themselves as a spiritual union in diversity?
2. What do they want to say to their brothers and sisters in the faith from other cultures?
3. What are the opportunities moving forward for building relationships and collaboration?

Although the Catholic Church may have some things to mend according to this letter, it's encouraging to see these Catholic leaders get together to wrestle with the elephant in the pew.

> There is another thing that disturbs me to no end about the American church. You have a white church and you have a Negro church. *You have allowed segregation to creep into the doors of the church. How can such a division exist in the true*

Body of Christ? You must face the tragic fact that when you stand at 11:00 on Sunday morning to sing "All Hail the Power of Jesus' Name" and "Dear Lord and Father of Mankind," you stand in the most segregated hour of Christian America. They tell me that there is more integration in the entertaining world and other secular agencies than there is in the Christian Church. How appalling that is [emphasis added].

If that statement doesn't disturb you, I pray that God gives you a burden for this issue to the point of disturbance. Dr. King had such foresight, as he was able to see that the entertainment world and other secular agencies would embrace diversity at a much more rapid rate than the Church. Unfortunately, God's Church has remained filled with a bunch of Christian separatists — Christians who separate, withdraw, and only worship with those who look similar to them.

I understand that there are a few Christians among you who try to justify segregation on the basis of the Bible. They argue that the Negro is inferior by nature because of Noah's curse upon the children of Ham. Oh my friends, this is blasphemy. This is against everything that the Christian religion stands for. I must say to you as I have said to so many Christians before, that in Christ "there is neither Jew nor Gentile, there is neither bond nor free, there is neither male nor female, for we are all one in Christ Jesus." Moreover, I must reiterate the words that I uttered on Mars Hill: "God that made the world and all things therein . . . hath made of one blood all nations of men for to dwell on all the face of the earth."

So, Americans, I must urge you to get rid of every aspect of segregation. The broad universalism standing at the center of the gospel makes both the theory and practice of segregation morally unjustifiable. Segregation is a blatant denial of the unity which we all have in Christ. It substitutes an "I-it" relationship for the "I-thou" relationship. The segregator relegates the segregated to the status of a thing rather than elevate him to the status of a person. The underlying philosophy of Christianity is diametrically opposed to the underlying philosophy of segregation, and all the dialectics of the logicians cannot make them lie down together.

I can't say anymore here. Read the last paragraph again. "I-it" vs. "I-thou." Segregation is simply not logical in a gospel-centric Christian context. MLK goes on to praise the Supreme Court's unanimous decision on May 17, 1954. It held that school segregation violated the Equal Protection and Due Process clauses of the Fourteenth Amendment.

> I praise your Supreme Court for rendering a great decision just two or three years ago. I am happy to know that so many persons of goodwill have accepted the decision as a great moral victory. But I understand that there are some brothers among you who have risen up in open defiance. I hear that their legislative halls ring loud with such words as "nullification" and "interposition." They have lost the true meaning of democracy and Christianity. So I would urge each of you to plead patiently with your brothers, and tell them that this isn't the way. With understanding goodwill, you are obligated to seek to change their attitudes. Let them know that in standing against integration, they are not only standing against the noble precepts of your democracy, but also against the eternal edicts of God Himself. Yes, America, there is still the need for an Amos to cry out to the nation: "Let judgment roll down as waters, and righteousness as a mighty stream."
>
> May I say just a word to those of you who are struggling against this evil. Always be sure that you struggle with Christian methods and Christian weapons. Never succumb to the temptation of becoming bitter. As you press on for justice, be sure to move with dignity and discipline, using only the weapon of love. Let no man pull you so low as to hate him. Always avoid violence. If you succumb to the temptation of using violence in your struggle, unborn generations will be the recipients of a long and desolate night of bitterness, and your chief legacy to the future will be an endless reign of meaningless chaos.
>
> In your struggle for justice, let your oppressor know that you are not attempting to defeat or humiliate him, or even to pay him back for injustices that he has heaped upon you. Let him know that you are merely seeking justice for him as well

as yourself. Let him know that the festering sore of segregation debilitates the white man as well as the Negro. With this attitude you will be able to keep your struggle on high Christian standards.

Many persons will realize the urgency of seeking to eradicate the evil of segregation. There will be many Negroes who will devote their lives to the cause of freedom. There will be many white persons of goodwill and strong moral sensitivity who will dare to take a stand for justice. Honesty impels me to admit that such a stand will require willingness to suffer and sacrifice. So don't despair if you are condemned and persecuted for righteousness' sake. Whenever you take a stand for truth and justice, you are liable to scorn. Often you will be called an impractical idealist or a dangerous radical. Sometimes it might mean going to jail. If such is the case you must honorably grace the jail with your presence. It might even mean physical death. But if physical death is the price that some must pay to free their children from a permanent life of psychological death, then nothing could be more Christian. Don't worry about persecution, America; you are going to have that if you stand up for a great principle. I can say this with some authority, because my life was a continual round of persecutions. After my conversion I was rejected by the disciples at Jerusalem. Later I was tried for heresy at Jerusalem. I was jailed at Philippi, beaten at Thessalonica, mobbed at Ephesus, and depressed at Athens. And yet I am still going. I came away from each of these experiences more persuaded than ever before that "neither death nor life, nor angels, nor principalities, nor things present, nor things to come . . . shall separate us from the love of God, which is in Christ Jesus our Lord." I still believe that standing up for the truth of God is the greatest thing in the world. This is the end of life. The end of life is not to be happy. The end of life is not to achieve pleasure and avoid pain. The end of life is to do the will of God, come what may.

Dr. King was advocating the concept that I have identified as Do the Right Thing Leadership. Do the right thing, because it's the right thing to do.

I must bring my writing to a close now. Timothy is waiting to deliver this letter, and I must take leave for another church. But just before leaving, I must say to you, as I said to the church at Corinth, that I still believe that love is the most durable power in the world. Over the centuries men have sought to discover the highest good. This has been the chief quest of ethical philosophy. This was one of the big questions of Greek philosophy. The Epicureans and the Stoics sought to answer it; Plato and Aristotle sought to answer it. What is the summum bonum of life? I think I have an answer, America. I think I have discovered the highest good. It is love. This principle stands at the center of the cosmos. As John says, "God is love." He who loves is a participant in the being of God. He who hates does not know God.

So American Christians, you may master the intricacies of the English language. You may possess all of the eloquence of articulate speech. But even if you "speak with the tongues of man and angels, and have not love, you are become as sounding brass, or a tinkling cymbal."

As Pastor Rick Warren stated in chapter 3, "Let us stop just saying we love each other; let us really show it by our actions" (1 John 3:18, NLT). We can talk a good act: "I love people." But do we really love them? Our love is revealed in how we act toward them. Pastors, leaders, young people, Christians, and those who are not yet believers — we must move beyond talking about love and *live love*! Why? The lyrical genius of the famous children's song has the answer: "the Bible tells me so!"

CHURCH DIVERSITY CHALLENGE 4

How do you feel about your own church and beliefs after reading Dr. King's letter?

In what ways did you feel that Dr. King's letter addressed some of the practices and beliefs of your own church?

In what ways do you feel the church has changed since the time of Dr. King? In what ways has it not changed?

What changes need to be made to your church based upon what you read in Dr. King's letter?

Endnotes

1. http://www.mlkonline.net/christians.html.
2. Ibid.
3. Dr. Joe Newman, *Race and the Assemblies of God Church* (Youngstown, NY: Cambria Press, 2007).
4. United States Conference of Catholic Bishops, 3-02-2010 press release.

5 Corporate America Cares More Than the Church

We're investing considerable time and resources today to develop tomorrow's leaders — with a committed eye toward ensuring those leaders bring different backgrounds, views, and experiences to their positions.

— Cindy Brinkley, AT&T Senior VP & Chief Diversity Officer

The only way race will become a non-issue is if we make race an issue.

— Scott Williams

Check out video 5
www.nlpg.com/churchdiversity

Being progressive and ahead of the times is probably not the best description of the Church. That's not meant as a slight against the Church, it's just the harsh reality that the business world is typically light years ahead of the Church in most areas. There are definitely some areas where corporate America needs to be the front-row pupil of the Church; however, diversity is not one of them.

Over the years, more and more churches have been implementing industry practices that help to advance their mission and share the gospel. In chapter 2 I shared some of those industry concepts from the business/leadership book *Good to Great*. This book has been widely adapted by ministry leaders around the globe as a critical component of the leadership and DNA of their church. It is definitely one of our valued resources at LifeChurch.tv. I think learning from industry practices is important, but of course I'm a guy that was in the business world prior to ministry. Maybe the way that I think is different and has been shaped by the fact that I've been in a leadership role at a church that has been voted by church peers as *Outreach Magazine*'s Most Innovative Church in America for the last three years in a row. LifeChurch.tv does an excellent job of leveraging technology, and using innovation and business models to effectively share the gospel and expand the reach and impact of the global Church. Although LifeChurch.tv is progressive, the leadership team is always in learning mode as they recognize they can always learn from some of today's top companies. My senior pastor, Craig Groeschel, and members of our Directional Leadership Team read many business leadership and organizational lifecycle books and apply the various concepts and principles to a ministry context. As a matter of fact, in the summer of 2010, I read through a list of books that Pastor Craig shared on his blog. Of the 12 books he entitled "Recent Reads" (*Sun Stand Still, Getting Things Done, How the Mighty Fall, The Upside of Irrationality, Predictably Irrational, The Big Short, Delivering Happiness, Just as I Am, Predictable Success, Radical, The War of Art*, and *Rework*), only 2 of those books would be considered Christian or ministry-related and the other 10 were more about business, leadership, organizational lifecycle, and productivity. Most of those were recent reads of mine, too. I love the boldness of Steven Furtick's *Sun Stand Still*, and one of my favorite reads is *The War of Art*. The bottom line is that the Church must be open to learning from the business world, and vice versa.

One fall afternoon I had lunch with my friend William, who runs an executive search firm. The firm's primary target group of candidates consists of high-level leaders for mega-churches. Learning that this type of industry existed was definitely new to me and is what I would consider a unique niche. I'm always intrigued and eager to learn from various business models and practices, so I began to ask William to share some of the effective strategies that his search firm is using, why those strategies work, and how their team went about developing them. (Of course I had my Moleskine notebook and iPhone on the table ready to jot down some good notes, ready to learn. I am always ready to take notes, ready to listen, ready to make mental notes, and ready to learn from any lunch, general meeting, or casual situation. I understand the value of L.L., which is short for "Listen and Learn.")

During the course of our conversation, William uttered one statement about what his company does and how they do it. He said (and I'm paraphrasing), "Scott, what we do is adapt the executive search practices of industry to the Church. Industry has been effectively doing this for years and as churches continue to grow, the importance of hiring the right person in the right leadership role is paramount. We conduct all of the research/assessment of both our client and the potential candidates, with our primary goal being to make a DNA match. Again, industry has been doing this for years and the church tends to be 10 to 15 years or so behind industry in many areas."

I will often use many of these business practices when I'm providing leadership and strategy consulting for various churches and ministry leaders.

I'm in total agreement with William's observation that the church tends to be 10 to 15 years behind industry in many areas, and one of those many areas is understanding the importance of embracing a culture of diversity. In an attempt to ascertain exactly what methods the business world has employed in creating work cultures that embrace diversity, I decided to do some research. I researched what the top diversity-leading corporations in the world were doing. Not only did I want to find out what they were doing, but also I wanted to clearly understand their philosophies and draw parallels to the Church. These parallels will help us to apply these corporate/business philosophies to the practices within the Church. I think one could argue that issues of race and diversity have made significant progress in most areas — sports, politics, music, culture, style, etc., but definitely not the Church. This is especially true in the United States. It's my hope that some of the practices learned from these corporations will help the Church to complete the circle of progress of race and diversity.

It wasn't very far into my research that I concluded that the *DiversityInc Magazine* was going to be a great resource. *DiversityInc* has phenomenal content and is an industry leader in understanding the aggregate result of diversity in the work place and its impact on the overall employee culture and the bottom line. *DiversityInc* puts together a yearly list of the top 50 companies for diversity in the world, based on some extensive criteria.[1] "The *DiversityInc* Top 50 Companies for Diversity list began in 2001, at the same time many corporations were beginning to understand the business value of diversity-management initiatives. Like diversity management itself, the list has evolved significantly and continues to be refined and improved to reflect how rapidly companies are adapting these strategies."

I researched this list and the various companies it featured. While conducting my research, I decided to utilize ten of the companies featured on the top ten list for 2009; however, there was a more recently released 2010 list. There was only a little movement in the list from 2009 and 2010, and I feel these ten companies selected will provide the appropriate clarity and learning. Again, the companies featured on this list are for the purposes of providing the Church, ministry leaders, general congregants, denominational leaders, and business leaders a blueprint of how to effectively utilize these industry standards to effect change in the heart and face of the Church. Learning from these corporations will help the Church to "move beyond the dream," from where it is to where it needs to be, and to make Sunday no longer the most-segregated day of the week.

I chose the number ten because ten is one of the perfect numbers and signifies *the perfection of divine order*. Again, observations from these corporations should spark some new thoughts and help to complete the full circle of doing our part in helping God's will to be done on earth as it is in heaven.

This chapter will identify the fact that corporate America cares more about diversity than the Church does. Although all of the criteria used in *DiversityInc*'s assessment does not directly apply to ministry leadership, the following are excerpts from the article along with observations about what the church can learn from these diversity-focused corporations.

#10 Company for Diversity: IBM Corporation. No company embodies values more globally than IBM. It's mentoring and training program as well as its employee groups reach across all borders to ensure inclusivity and enable this corporate giant to reach and connect with all employees, clients, and communities.

Diversity strengths: IBM has increased its emphasis on substantive cross-cultural training and talent development with a definite global emphasis. Chairman, President, and CEO Samuel Palmisano is directly involved in how IBM approaches diversity. IBM's board also reflects its diversity. The 12-member board has two black members, one Latino member, and one Asian member.

IBM Vice President of Diversity and WorkForce Programs Ron Glover says, "Global work-force diversity is a cornerstone of IBM's strategy to differentiate itself as one of the world's great companies, and that's especially important during challenging economic times. IBM remains fully committed to a culture of diversity and inclusiveness as an essential part of how we attract and retain the best people around the world. An inclusive workplace makes for a creative environment; IBM believes this and will continue to promote global work-force diversity regardless of the economic climate."

There are several things that stand out about IBM in their approach to diversity that we can relate to the Church. Cross-cultural training, diversity as a core value, the diversity in their governing board, and the fact that the CEO is directly involved in diversity issues are just a few. The Church must develop training programs that are culturally sensitive and openly discuss issues of race and ethnicity. The Church is generally silent on developing cultural sensitivity training because it's easier to pretend that the problem doesn't exist. Training is where it all begins, even if there is just some basic training for all new hires and existing employees. An in-house person, on-line trainer, or a sub-contractor can lead this training. The only way these trainings will be accepted or viewed as credible is if the senior leader is involved in diversity discussions. Involvement doesn't mean doing all of the work or changing the mission statement, but it means the senior leader learns to have a heart that beats for diversity. The initial thrust toward diversity begins and ends with the senior leader. In many denominations, the church board has more influence than the senior leader; therefore, it's important to look at the make-up of the board. If the board is a bunch of old guys and gals that look like one another and are related to a "legend" in the church, that's a problem. IBM understands that diversity in the boardroom is crucial. Unfortunately, this thought has not fully transitioned to the Church.

It may take time; however, the intentionality will begin to make a difference over time. In January of 2010, *Time Magazine* released an article about Pastor Bill Hybels (senior pastor of Willow Creek Church in Chicago, Illinois) and his journey with the issues of church diversity, titled "Can Mega Churches Bridge the Racial Divide?" The article discusses Hybels' personal growth and leadership in the area of racial reconciliation and church diversity. A section of the article mentions the fact that an African American recently joined Willow's elder board. Curtis Sallee, a black 15-year "Creeker," comments, "What Bill has done racially has been nothing less than miraculous. There needs to be someone who speaks for the church, a teaching pastor or staff, who's a minority. That's the next step. I don't know whether they are ready to take it. But they're going to have to address it sooner or later." If you have a recent board member who is already thinking about creating forward-moving steps for the church without the right people involved in the discussion process, the discussion will only go so far. Additionally, Willow Creek's story should be encouragement that this type of change doesn't happen overnight; however, it does happen. It just takes time.

Assess → Believe → Change!

#9 Company for Diversity: Coca-Cola. Coca-Cola's deep-rooted commitment to creating an inclusive work force has been increasingly evident since the soft drink giant settled the largest racial-discrimination lawsuit in history and really took stock of what diversity stood for and the type of employer it wanted to be.

Diversity strengths: President and CEO Muhtar Kent is following in the footsteps of his predecessor, E. Neville Isdell, and is setting the bar high for a company with absolute values of integrity and inclusiveness. As a global corporate entity, this is especially important to Coca-Cola. Chief Diversity Officer Steve Bucherati has ensured that employees are engaged and involved in diversity efforts via in-depth training, including such programs as "Breaking Down the Barriers: Challenge Day," which is the corporate version of a nationally recognized diversity training program that has been launched in schools across the country. The emphasis on diversity is reflected in the company's demographics. For example, Coca-Cola's management is 31.8 percent black, Latino, Asian, and American Indian. The company also has a long and impressive history of philanthropic contributions to multicultural groups, with 26 percent of its total philanthropic budget going to various diverse organizations.

One of the many things the Church can learn from Coca-Cola is that you don't have to be on the wrong side of a discrimination lawsuit or spend years ignoring the issues of diversity before you recognize that you need to make some changes. If you have done a poor or even non-existent job of addressing diversity and are uncomfortable addressing the issue, don't beat yourself up. Be willing to make the necessary changes to improve the current condition of your church. Just as Coca-Cola had to take an honest assessment of what they stood for and then made necessary adjustments, ministry leaders and congregants should do the same. Coca-Cola can proudly boast the slogan of "America's Real Choice." Do we think that Coke's success might be due to the fact that they truly want to make Coke disciples of all nations? They want everyone to drink the Coca-Cola "Kool-Aid." They legitimately are the real thing! Coca-Cola is selling carbonated sugar water and the Church is promoting opportunities for the Living Water.

If you were to make an honest assessment of your church, would you say it was the real thing when it comes to embracing diversity, or would your church be more defined by simply tolerating diversity? Asking that question and providing an honest assessment is a great start. We will talk more about assessment in the final chapter of this book.

Church leaders shouldn't feel awful if they haven't done anything to allow church diversity to be raised as a point of legitimate conversation. There is only a very small percent of churches and ministry leaders who have been audacious enough to address this topic. It's never too late. Coca Cola didn't respond adequately until they were in the largest discrimination lawsuit in history. That wasn't too late for Coca-Cola. In fact, it happened to be right on time.

Assess → Believe → Change!

#8 Company for Diversity: Merck. Merck has a history as a diversity leader as evidenced by its presence on *DiversityInc*'s Top 50 list for the seventh year in a row. The pharmaceutical company moved up significantly in 2009, largely because of its demonstrable CEO commitment and strong employee resource groups.

Diversity strengths: Merck's diversity efforts are led by Vice President and Chief Diversity Officer Deborah Dagit, who has become a well-regarded global diversity leader. Merck has been a trendsetter in creating an inclusive work force. Chairman, President, and CEO Richard T. Clark is a strong advocate of diversity. He personally signs off on executive compensation tied to diversity as well as goals and achievements for supplier diversity. Clark's ten direct reports (all high-ranking leaders) reflect his commitment to diversity — three are black, one is Asian, and one is Native American. The company has a long history of philanthropic commitment to multicultural groups. Merck also has an improving supplier diversity program. This year, the company spent 8.6 percent of its total Tier I (direct contractor) procurement with minority-business enterprises (MBEs).

Clark shared his viewpoint on diversity with the following comment: "Embracing diversity and inclusion is not only the right thing to do; it is an important part of our business strategy and key to the long-term success of Merck. The incorporation of these principles into our business enables us to drive innovation and create the next generation of lifesaving and enhancing products for patients who need them."

Someone with vision and commitment like this is the poster child for church diversity and "Do the Right Thing Leadership." If the CEO of a pharmaceutical company has the internal values and mindset that embracing diversity is the right thing to do, shouldn't God's house and its leaders take that same position?

In his book *Courageous Leadership*, Pastor Bill Hybels said, "The local church is the hope of the world and its future rests primarily in the hand of its leaders."[2] If the Church's business strategy is to go into the entire world, spread the gospel, make disciples of *all nations*, and lead people to Jesus, it's absolutely necessary for the hands of church leaders to reach out and grab onto the position that the Merck CEO has taken. Not only is embracing diversity the right thing to do, but it should be an important part of the Church's business strategy. As the world continues to get smaller and racial lines continue to blur, the Church must recognize diversity as being the future and the key for the long-term success of the Church.

One of the best ways to drive innovation is to have a diverse group of people be a part of the dreaming process. If ministry leaders all look alike, think alike, and have similar backgrounds, they're missing out on an important piece of the innovation driver. Here is how Chairman Clark drives it home. He states, "The incorporation of these principles into our business enables us to drive innovation and create the next generation of lifesaving and enhancing products for patients who need them."

The Church has patients whose lives need to be saved, and a church with a monolithic platform, staff, and congregation might be an inhibiting factor for those who are in need of the living water — not Coca-Cola, but Jesus. People are dying and going to hell and God's chosen vessel of the local church is sitting on the sidelines. It's time to get in the game! The Church must be the entity that people look to for solutions, innovations, and answers.

Let's be honest, if you were looking for someone to help you in the area of computer technology, would you go to someone who was stuck in the 1980s, still using a typewriter like Uncle Ricoh from *Napoleon Dynamite*? Absolutely not! The same is true for the Church. If you are looking for a new life, something different, something fresh, and something real, are you going to feel comfortable in an institution whose heart is stuck in a pre-civil rights movement era as it relates to race and ethnicity? Absolutely not! This current generation and generations to come want diversity and expect diversity. It's time that the "hope of the world," the local church, meets those real needs.

Merck Vice President and Chief Diversity Officer Deborah Dagit made a statement that is so applicable to the Church. Not only is it applicable to the Church, but many ministry leaders should probably repent after truly digesting what she said. Dagit said, "In a modern global business, the integration of diversity principles and practices are required elements. Our work force and our marketplace expect us to be not just culturally aware but culturally competent in how we engage both our employees and our customers. A failure to embrace diversity is a signal to your talent and your consumer that you are out of touch with the current realities of doing business."

The Church is out of touch with the realities of reaching all people for Jesus, and the sad thing is that many ministry leaders don't even realize it. It's time for the Church to realize that the integration of diversity and culturally competent practices are required elements. The people who come through the doors of a church expect the church to be different. They expect the church to not just be culturally aware, but culturally competent in how it engages staff, community, and attendees.

It is a travesty for the living, breathing chosen vessel of God to be out of touch. The only way that the Church can get in touch is to grab a hold and begin to address this sticky topic known as church diversity. Merck drives innovation by having a diverse group of people at the leadership table. Who's at your table?

Assess → Believe → Change!

#7 Company for Diversity: Kaiser Permanente. Kaiser Permanente, a managed care consortium, has been a diversity leader for many years and is the type of company others quietly sought out for diversity advice and best practices. Kaiser's surge on the "Top 50 Companies for Diversity" list is indicative of its increasing ability to let the world in on what makes it such a great model for diversity. Kaiser Permanente's commitment to diversity is so deep it has impacted the way it addresses its customers' health needs.

Diversity strengths: Chairman and CEO George C. Halvorson is a major diversity supporter and ties 10 percent of his ten direct reports' bonuses to diversity goals. With the help of Senior Vice President and Chief Diversity Officer Ronald Knox, Halvorson has created an inclusive work force that is reflected in its demographics. Kaiser Permanente's work force is 56.9 percent black, Asian, Latino, and American Indian. This diversity carries over into its management, including the highest ranks. Of those in the category of "CEO and direct reports," 33.4 percent are black, Asian, and Latino, and 42.9 percent are women. The company also has one of the most diverse boards anywhere, with 21 percent black, 14.5 percent Latino, and 14.5 percent Asian American. Kaiser Permanente has also developed work/life programs and very strong diversity training.

Kaiser CEO Ron Halvorson says, "Our diversity is one of our greatest strengths. It creates synergy, productivity, and the ability for us to serve a diverse world. That is even truer in challenging economic times. The factors that drive our embrace of diversity as a strategic operating frame — the diversity of our customer base, the diversity of the labor market and our work force, the moral imperative — do not cease to exist in times of economic challenge. Neither can our commitment to diversity."

Halvorson's comment about diversity creating synergy and allowing Kaiser to serve a diverse world is a brilliant perspective for the Church. Having diverse · perspectives allows for increased productivity and a better ability to serve a lost and broken world. Halvorson made it clear that Kaiser will not sacrifice its commitment to diversity even during tough economic times.

The Church can sometimes get into the business mindset and shallow thinking that if they try to reach a particular ethnic demographic, they will potentially minimize their GPA (Giving Per Attendee). It's refreshing to hear a corporate CEO utter these words about morality with a moral imperative, "The moral imperative . . . [does] not cease to exist in times of economic challenge."

The moral imperative of the Church and Jesus' mandate to go into *all of the world* and share the good news with *all nations* does not cease to exist because of a struggling economy or because churches need to raise money, hire staff, or fund a building campaign. God honors a heart that truly desires to reach "all people," even if the "all people" happen to not look like what the senior pastor or the congregants are used to seeing.

Kaiser Senior Vice President and Chief Diversity Officer Ronald Knox echoed those same sentiments when he said, "Challenging economic situations cannot be the determinant of diversity commitment; otherwise, progress toward institutionalizing diversity-driven strategies and solutions, and achieving progress toward social justice, erode and revive with the ebb and flow of economic dynamics. This practice does not sustain and promote diversity as an essential and guiding philosophy in business and society."

Both of these senior leaders have an unwavering commitment to making diversity a priority. You can tell from the tone of their language and the diversity measurables/metrics that they have put in place that their commitment is a commitment of the heart, and that is what's needed in the Church. The commitment of the heart will lead to appropriate systems, conversations, and prayers, which will ultimately lead to the beautiful doors of diversity in the Church being opened. Commitment is critical.

Assess → Believe → Change!

#6 Company for Diversity: Sodexo. Sodexo's steady rise up the "Top 50 Companies for Diversity List" in recent years and its increasing reputation as a trendsetting diversity leader are attributable to a strong CEO commitment from past President and CEO Dick Macedonia and current President and CEO George Chavel, and the powerful impact of Senior Vice President and Global Chief Diversity Officer Rohini Anand. She has become a global thought leader in diversity management and a forceful voice for improvement both internally and externally.

Diversity strengths: Sodexo, one of the largest food service and facilities management companies in the world, is the best company on the Top 50 list for understanding and using metrics. Its emphasis on understanding the "Return on Investment (ROI)" of each undertaking is even more valuable in tight economic times. Over the past five years, the company has developed an integrated metrics platform to assess diversity behavior and values at all levels, including the C-suite (chief officers COO, CEO, and CIO). Sodexo tells us there are four specific areas: diversity training metrics, which includes a satisfaction survey and a follow-up survey six months later to managers to determine behavior change; an employee engagement survey, analyzed by demographic groups; the identification of how C-suite executives are demonstrating Sodexo's diversity values and behaviors through a 360-assessment; and the Sodexo diversity index. This index is a scorecard that tracks both quantitative and qualitative results by measuring and rewarding outcomes as well as efforts.

What immediately stands out about Sodexo is the recognition of the role that the past President and CEO Dick Macedonia's leadership played in influencing current CEO and President George Chavel. Chavel continued to champion diversity efforts and maintains Sodexo's status as an industry leader for diversity. If you apply this to the Church, you can only imagine the reduplication effects of future church leaders and congregations around the globe.

Imagine church planters and established church successors realizing the importance of and embracing the core value of diversity. There is a trickle-down effect that would lead youth pastors, children's pastors, and next generation ministry leaders to pour these values into the up-and-coming generation of world changers. Thousands of church planters would enter into their unique church-planting scenarios with not necessarily the desire to be a multiethnic church, but the desire to lead a church that embraces the core value of diversity. This reality is totally attainable, but not without ministry leaders simulating leadership philosophies like Sodexo CEO Chavel. Not only do you embrace diversity, but you should also put systems in place to appropriately measure the outcomes. Metrics do one thing: they demonstrate what you value. You measure what you value.

At LifeChurch.tv we measure a number of things that impact our mission of leading people to become fully devoted followers of Christ. Not only do we do 360 degree assessments, we measure things like attendance, giving, number of LifeGroups (small groups), number of salvations, number of baptisms, giving per attendee, number of volunteers, number of students, number of kids, and the list goes on. One thing that has been true about LifeChurch.tv's metrics is that they have evolved over the last several years. The core values are the same, but how we value and assess the attainment of those identified values has changed. At the end of 2009 we decided that we wanted to raise more volunteer leaders in the Body of Christ at our individual campuses, so the metrics began to shift. The focus wasn't on the number of small groups, attendance, or volunteers, but rather the number of "leaders" and "leaders of leaders."

The same is true for measuring for diversity. If diversity is one of your core values, then you will measure it in some shape, form, or fashion as you would attendance, giving, and number of volunteers. You might start by measuring whether or not you even have a diversity plan. I will talk more about this in the final chapter that outlines the ABCs of church diversity.

Externally, Sodexo is first-rate in the way it communicates its diversity. Its website also receives a perfect score for its consistent and very visible diversity message in both words and images. Sodexo also allocates 35 percent of its advertising budget to multicultural media. Clearly, both Anand and Chavel are strong ambassadors for diversity. President Chavel understands how embracing diversity helps Sodexo keep a competitive advantage as he states, "It is all about maintaining a competitive advantage. We know, and research has proven, that diversity drives innovation. Now more than ever, we need to have the best and brightest talent thinking about how we can deliver value to the customers we serve. We have made a very deliberate decision to continue to invest in our people and their development. This includes our employee network groups, mentoring initiatives, and professional development opportunities for our people."

Diversity drives innovation. If you want the brightest, best, and most capable staff and leaders involved with your church, diversity must be a core value. People want to be challenged but realize that those challenges come from people who have a totally different perspective than they do. Shouldn't the Church want the best and the brightest? If the answer is yes, I would hypothesize that the best and brightest don't all look like you or me. As I look at pockets of staff teams within LifeChurch.tv and other churches, there is no way you can convince me that there were no minority candidates that were "the best and brightest" to fill certain roles. Of the 14 LifeChurch.tv campuses — all different sizes — there are only two locations that have at least one-third of their staff team represented by minorities. They are both campuses with several thousand people and happen to be in Oklahoma City — my campus (NW Oklahoma City) and the South Oklahoma City campus led by Trevor Williams. Trevor is actually my brother — no, not really. Trevor is a big bald-headed white guy who played football as a lineman at Oklahoma State University. Trevor has a huge heart of gold, which has translated into the heart of a leader who truly embraces diversity.

Research has proven that diversity drives innovation. The fact that Sodexo scored a perfect score on its website shows that they understand that you never get a second chance to make a first impression. Websites and print material should be inclusive and appear to embrace diversity.

I remember our student ministry doing a big invite push around Valentine's Day. The printed invite cards were similar to the cards you would receive on Valentine's Day as a child. My youth pastor specifically asked for those cards to take into account that 50 percent of the students in our student ministry were black. When we received the cards they had white boys, white girls, and an image of a bear on them. My youth pastors felt like it was a big miss and that the cards communicated that we didn't take our attendees or any minorities into consideration. I love the fact that they saw it that way. It demonstrated that they had grown to have hearts that are sensitive to and truly embrace diversity. Ensuring your media and print embrace diversity doesn't mean you have to have the iStockphoto of every race being featured, but rather it means being thoughtful and communicating a desire to reach all people. Having any minority represented is ten times better than having none represented.

Assess → Believe → Change!

#5 Company for Diversity: PricewaterhouseCoopers. Pricewaterhouse-Coopers (PwC) was the first of the major accounting firms to become a national diversity leader. What's truly remarkable about PwC is their relentless pursuit of diversity management excellence and their deep comprehension that diversity is a quickly evolving discipline and that in order to succeed they need to be constantly improving.

Diversity strengths: The firm clearly understands the importance of diversity to its direct lines of business and in recent years has named critical line partners to the post of chief diversity officer. The current CDO, Roy Weathers, is a tax partner and one of U.S. Chairman and Senior Partner Dennis Nally's seven direct reports. PwC definitely values branding its diversity commitment as a key trigger for recruitment, retention, talent development, client acquisition and retention, community development, and supplier diversity. The firm's website and internal and external communications consistently reflect the importance of diversity in every aspect of its business. The work force demographics also demonstrate that commitment. For a company in professional services, having new hires that are 31 percent Asian, black, Latino, and American Indian and 51.6 percent women is commendable. The company continues its demographic diversity even at the highest levels. Of Nally's direct reports, one is black and one is Asian.

PwC is number one in "The *DiversityInc* Top 10 Global Diversity Companies" list for its deep-rooted commitment to inclusiveness in all its operations worldwide, including company-sanctioned global employee resource groups and working globally to change laws perceived as oppressive. The firm also surveys its employees on diversity through focus groups, exit interviews, point-of-view dialogues, and national and local meetings with management that includes town halls with Nally.

Many churches have some sort of exit interview process for employees, and if they don't, they should. This is a great way to get that candid feedback when employees leave for various reasons. Exit interviews will generally draw out the good, bad, and ugly, as employees feel free to be 100 percent honest. I have yet to see or hear of a church exit interview process or any annual review process that includes questions about how well a church performed in the area of commitment to diversity. At LifeChurch.tv we have adopted and assimilated the Gallup 12-question survey. This survey has some great questions that have been slightly modified to fit within LifeChurch.tv cultural terminology. Maybe surveys like this, used to determine employee engagement, could have a diversity component. Maybe our annual review questions or 360-degree survey questions could also take diversity into consideration. When your church or organization is determining questions to include in your annual evaluation process, include a question about diversity. Is diversity a value to your organization? Is diversity a value to your team?

The reality is that if church staff, volunteers, and leadership do not make this an area of priority, it will never become a priority. This lack of interest will trickle down throughout the congregation. Again, the process of including a diversity question can be as simple as a question like this: "Do you feel that XYZ church made a commitment to creating a culture that valued diversity in its staff, congregants, or outreach?" A question as broad-reaching as this one will allow churches at various stages of progress on the diversity continuum to be able to demonstrate progress. Although diversity may be a slow and difficult process for your church, there is one thing that can happen at a much swifter rate. Another way to create diversity synergy is to develop racially diverse ministry partners to work alongside your church.

PwC has a long history of giving back to the community. Eighteen percent of its philanthropic budget goes to multicultural organizations. They have also increased supplier diversity efforts and are working with suppliers to help them understand how to do business with the Big 4 accounting firms (the four largest international accounting firms: PwC, Ernst & Young, Deloitte, and KPMG). Most churches give both time and resources to other non-profits, outreaches, ministries, and mission efforts. As it relates to church diversity, ministry leaders should look at the percent of their personal outreach and philanthropic budget that goes toward local multicultural organizations. I'm not implying that a church should cut their international missions budget, but what I am saying is to "look local." Church organizations can make great strides in impacting church diversity by exposing their congregations to local multicultural partnerships and outreach. Find multicultural organizations to give to, partner with, and work alongside. When Jesus said go into all the world, that didn't simply mean go around the globe. For many churches, that can essentially refer to going around the corner and across the train tracks.

There are so many historic and personal illustrations for me in regard to going to the other side of the train tracks. For those of you who may not understand what that means, most communities were and some still are racially segregated by a set of train tracks or a dividing street. It can be "the Hood" on one side of the tracks, with things getting a little nicer, cleaner, and newer on the other side. Hood or not, many times there is just a clear racial divide. My wife and I spent some time with the leaders of one of our LifeChurch.tv network churches, the H20 Church in Ardmore, Oklahoma, my wife's hometown. Ardmore is about 100 miles from Oklahoma City in a rural but growing area. During their leadership retreat, LaKendria and I shared our heart and passion for church diversity. The senior pastor of this rural church, Chuck McKinnel, developed a heart to reach across the train tracks. Their church is at the genesis of the change process; remember, it begins with the heart of the senior leader.

I had hooked up one of our promising young students, Forrest, with an internship at H20 Church. Forrest happens to be bi-racial, half black and half white. During his internship, Forrest was in awe of the fact that the town of Ardmore was literally separated by a set of train tracks. He said, "Pastor Scott, I didn't know that a town could literally be divided by a set of train tracks. I thought that was a figure of speech." H20 Church has a long way to go and is experiencing minor traction in the area of diversity; however, the leader of this church of approximately 300 people in rural Oklahoma is trying. They are primed to move their church from where it is to where it needs to be.

On January 12, 2010, the world was impacted by one of the most devastating natural disasters of our time. Haiti was hit by an earthquake with a 7.0 magnitude, leaving hundreds of thousands of people dead and thousands upon thousands of orphans in one of the poorest countries in the world. This was another instance where people were exposed to a culture that they only knew existed from afar via infomercials of Haitian children eating some porridge-like food, with flies buzzing around their heads. The realness of the earthquake and the reaching out of millions of Americans has changed the game. People who had never even remotely thought about adopting a "black" or Haitian child now wanted to help and adopt. I remember my wife and I sitting in the living room with our LifeGroup (small group) that meets every Wednesday. We were talking about the earthquake and how watching everything happening in Haiti had changed everyone's context. One 30-year-old white female, Rachelle, had been reading online, in addition to watching everything on television, and she cried for several days. It moved her to the level of considering adopting a Haitian baby. It was something that clicked as God grabbed her heart and totally changed her context. Everyone else in the group was touched and inspired by the earthquake in different fashions.

These interactions that churches have with diverse groups are going to garner different types of responses from the leaders and congregants. The guaranteed outcome of these interactions is that people will be impacted and their context will begin to change. Adoption is really changing the context. I remember doing a radio interview about my book and leadership on Grounded Radio with Toben Heim and Ryan Dobson. Ryan is the son of Dr. James Dobson, founder and chairman of Focus on the Family, a global-reaching non-profit organization. They were talking about how adoption of black and minority children in general has affected their diversity context. I hear this over and over, as families are not just having friends of different races but are growing up with brothers and sisters of different races and sons and daughters of different races. The Church must be sensitive to the fact that the new blended family is not just about the divorced and re-married. The new blended family is a family consisting of multiple races within the same family unit. Is your church family prepared to embrace, understand, and shepherd the new blended family?

PwC U.S. Chairman and Senior Partner Dennis Nally understands that in order to attract and retain the best and brightest talent, their "commitment to diversity has not wavered during this incredibly challenging time for our country, our global economy, and for each of our businesses. While we must focus on the immediate and burning challenges we and our clients are facing in today's environment, we also understand that we must continue to attract, retain, and develop the best talent, particularly our diverse talent. That talent will be the key driver in maintaining our competitiveness in the marketplace. In fact, I believe that our focus on diversity positions us to emerge from this downturn even stronger than before."

If the Church wants to attract, retain, and develop the best talent, diversity must be a value. If the Church wants to stay competitive in the marketplace of leading people to Jesus, diversity must be a value. The Church can't simply talk about taking the gospel to impoverished people around the world, when we can't worship with people across the tracks. If the Church wants to be in the business of leading people to Christ, diversity must be a value. If the Church wants to be competitive in economic downturns, diversity must be a value. If the Church wants to be stronger than ever before, diversity must be a value. If the Church doesn't want to be the only major institution stuck in the pre-civil rights movement era, diversity must be a value.

Assess → Believe → Change!

#4 Company for Diversity: Marriot. From the deep and public commitment of Chairman and CEO J. W. (Bill) Marriott Jr. to the longstanding culturally competent customer service, to the remarkable community-building supplier diversity and hotel-franchise program, Marriott is the textbook definition of a great company devoted to diversity. Improvement in the face of tough economic times is even greater proof of that.

Diversity strengths: Chairman and CEO J.W. Marriott Jr. is a visible force for diversity both in the company and out, serving as a member of the Executive Leadership Cabinet for the Martin Luther King Jr. National Memorial Project Foundation and honorary co-chair of the American Foundation for the Blind's Helen Keller Achievement Awards. He signs off personally on executive compensation tied to diversity, which accounts for 13 percent of the bonuses of his six direct reports. He also chairs the company's internal diversity council, which meets quarterly. He will also be one of the featured CEOs at the *DiversityInc* Top 50 CEO event.

Marriott has a diverse work force in the hospitality industry, featuring blacks, Latinos, Asians, and American Indians, which make up 60.4 percent of their U.S. work force. Management demographics are also very diverse. To make sure all its employees are culturally competent when dealing with customers from all backgrounds, Marriott has mandatory diversity training offered every month. Marriott's commitment to building hotels in urban areas and creating jobs, especially for black and Latino people in low-income communities, is unsurpassed. Marriott pledged to spend $1 billion with minority-business enterprises by 2010, and already has nearly doubled that goal.

There are a number of things that Marriot does well that the Church can learn from. It begins with the diversity of staff that you will find in any Marriot Hotel, no matter what part of the country you're in. This diverse employee group doesn't only include the desk clerk and cleaning crews, but there are diverse groups of high-level executive leaders within the Marriot organization. Many churches have some sort of bonus or flex-pay structure tied to their executive level leadership team members' performance. It would be great to see churches begin to have their bonus or flex-pay structure tied to diversity in some shape, form, or fashion. This doesn't mean you're being an extremist on the whole church diversity concept, but rather it means that leaders will be at least forced to think about diversity, begin discussions about diversity, and begin to make the changes necessary to change the face of the Church. You reward what you value!

Lastly, J.W. Marriot Jr. himself chairs the diversity council, and this degree of involvement is a must for the senior leadership in the Church. The senior leadership should be involved in the diversity discussion at some level.

Senior Vice President of External Affairs and Global Diversity Officer Jimmie Paschall said, "Our business is all about people. That's why we view our 'spirit to serve' culture of more than 80 years as a source of strength that our competitors can't easily replicate. We strive to create an inclusive environment where the talents and unique ideas of 300,000 employees at our managed and franchised properties worldwide can flourish. When our employees feel respected and valued, we know that they'll make our guests, suppliers, owners, and franchisees feel the same way, too. This is more than a philosophy — it's a strategy that works." If a successful organization with over 300,000 employees around the globe can embrace and understand the importance of diversity, shouldn't the local church? To put this in perspective, the largest church in the United States has less than 50,000 people who attend on a weekly basis. Marriot has over 300,000 employees. I believe Global Diversity Officer Paschall hits the nail on the head when he talks about "the spirit to serve" culture that can't be replicated by competitors. Inspired by Paschall's words above, let's relate his thoughts to how the Church can view diversity strategy: "When people of all races and ethnicities feel respected, valued, and embraced in the Church, we know they will make their friends, family, and *the least of these* feel the same way, too. This is more than some 'church diversity' philosophy, it's a strategy that will prove to change the heart and face of the Church."

Assess → Believe → Change!

#3 Company for Diversity: Ernst & Young. Ernst & Young, one of the largest professional services/accounting firms, has moved up the list substantially this year from number 17 in 2008. The reason is its clear focus on embedding diversity and inclusion in all of its global lines of business. The company's emphasis on strong talent development has paid off in a dedicated managerial/professional work force with a substantial pipeline to senior leadership.

Diversity strengths: Steve Howe, Americas area managing partner, is known as a strong public diversity advocate. The appointment last year of Billie Williamson as Ernst & Young's Americas inclusiveness officer has brought new depths to the diversity programs based on her history of advocating within the company for traditionally underrepresented groups.

Ernst & Young has a remarkable mentoring program, and all of its managers are involved as mentors/mentees in some way. Williamson has been involved in the development of several programs that add substantially to the company's ability to nurture talent.

Diversity training is mandatory for the entire work force. It lasts more than a full day and is held every month. Additionally, 20 percent of the firm's philanthropy goes to multicultural organizations, including the National Association of Black Accountants, the Association of Latino Professionals in Finance and Accounting, the Human Rights Campaign, and Acend, formerly known as the National Asian American Society of Accountants.

Ernst & Young has two primary strategies for diversity: training and mentoring. We have looked at training strategies in several of the other corporations; however, the mentoring concept is unique. In the church world, ministry leaders are challenged to have an accountability relationship, and many leaders are challenged to have mentoring relationships. You can take these relationships to a whole new level when you try to have at least one multicultural relationship. This is true for both ministry leaders and congregants and it's great 21st-century practice. Unfortunately, people dumb down having a relationship with someone that doesn't look like them to making statements like these: "I have black friends, I know several people that are black, I have a pair of black boots, and I even have a colored TV." (Not sure if you can laugh out loud while writing a book, but I just did.)

Howe was quoted as saying, "Our clients expect us to bring diverse teams and thinking to help solve their problems. Given the challenges companies are facing in the current economy, they need those diverse perspectives now more than ever. Our diversity and inclusiveness efforts have remained front and center, and that is not going to change. Our competitiveness now, and in the years to come, depends on it."

Mentoring relationships with a diverse group of people will help to develop those diverse perspectives. Ministry leaders should have three types of mentoring relationships, and at least one of these relationships should be a multicultural relationship. The purpose of having one of these relationships be diverse is to help broaden one's sense of diversity and appreciation for diversity.

Diversity has always been a passion for me; you could even refer to me as "Mr. Diversity." Even though I am supposed to be Mr. Diversity, I am still learning every day from my mentoring relationships. I have a mentoring relationship with an East Indian guy who has taught me much about Indian culture and beliefs, and even shattered the naive stereotype that all East Indians are Hindu. Jayson, whom I featured earlier in the book, use to be my children's pastor, and our relationship has broadened my overall perspective. Through natural conversations, I have become well informed about Indian culture, and it has impacted me personally in ways that are difficult to put into words. My other mentoring relationship is with my associate pastor, Robert Davis. Robert is considered "Old Man Wisdom" at the youthful age of 50 by my young team because of both his age and the overall life experience and wisdom he brings to the table. Robert grew up in an era in which he experienced school integration and forced busing. I always love Robert's insight and he loves how the value of diversity on our staff has personally shaped him. Our relationship has been mutually beneficial. Through our mentoring relationship, my perspective changes daily. *Change your perspective, change the game!*

Diversity in Mentoring

The three types of diversity mentoring relationships are as follows:

Be a Barnabas. Barnabas was the son of encouragement. He was always looking for someone to encourage, and encouragement was simply his nature. It's important for true disciples of Christ to encourage those around them, those they work with, and those they are responsible for. People tend to become what the most important people in their lives think they will become. Encourage someone today: *be a Barnabas*!

Seek Out a Paul. It's important that we all seek out a "Paul" to pour into our lives. This mentoring relationship can begin with observing individuals with qualities that you would like to see instilled within yourself. The initial mentoring relationship can occur from afar, simply by observing. At some point it's important for the individual who is seeking out his or her Paul to ask that person to be his or her mentor. I have had people ask me directly, "Will you be a Paul in my life?" After "the ask" has occurred it's important to sit down and line out expectations for the mentoring relationship. *Seek out a Paul!*

Pour into a Timothy. Just as Paul trained up and poured into Timothy, it's important for disciples of Christ, especially leaders in the church, to find a Timothy to pour into. *Pour into a Timothy!*

These relationships, coupled with a commitment to have at least one of them be racially, culturally, or ethnically diverse, will prove to be an asset to the Church. These diverse relationships will help to develop strong, well-rounded, and independent thinkers. Different types of iron really sharpen different types of iron. Ernst & Young Americas Inclusiveness Officer Billie Williamson talked about the importance of developing these types of thinkers when she said, "Now more than ever, we need people who think about familiar problems in new ways and who reject groupthink. We know that harnessing the strength of our inclusive culture is a competitive advantage."

Assess → Believe → Change!

#2 Company for Diversity: AT&T. Now that the mergers of AT&T, SBC Communications, Bell South, and Cingular have been successfully integrated, AT&T has re-emerged as the national diversity champion it should be. The company's long history as a national diversity leader and as a major recruiter of blacks, Latinos, and Asians deems it very worthy of this high spot on the list.

Diversity strengths: Chairman, CEO, and President Randall Stephenson is a vocal proponent of the business case for diversity, from a prominent quote on the corporate giant's website to his recent elevation to chairman of the NAACP Corporate Centennial Campaign. While Chief Diversity Officer Cindy Brinkley does not report directly to Stephenson, she has constant access to him and his "door is always open for diversity issues." Stephenson personally chairs the company's internal diversity council, which meets quarterly.

Having someone identified in the church that's either a lay leader or on staff to have direct access to the senior leader on diversity issues is very important. AT&T specifies that the person doesn't have to directly report to the senior leader as long as the "door is always open for diversity issues." AT&T's work force is as diverse as the U.S. customer base its serves. Employees are 39 percent black, Latino, Asian, and American Indian, while new hires are 49 percent black, Latino, Asian, and American Indian, demonstrating significant progress. Managers reflect this racial/ethnic diversity as well, since 30 percent of the company's managers are black, Latino, Asian, and American Indian. Even in these difficult times, the company demonstrates unbiased retention of its employees and managers, meaning it retains people at the same level, regardless of race, ethnicity, or gender.

AT&T is a very strong communicator of its belief in the importance of diversity. The company receives a perfect score for the way it displays diversity on its corporate website. The company also continues to be a leader in supplier diversity, a diversity discipline that really started with the telecoms. The company spends 9.6 percent of its total procurement with Tier I suppliers (direct contractors) who are minority- or women-owned businesses. The head of supplier diversity reports to the head of procurement, and AT&T has 16 employees dedicated to its supplier diversity efforts. The company also provides mentoring and financial assistance/education for its diverse suppliers.

Chairman, CEO, and President Randall L. Stephenson was quoted as saying, "Focusing on diversity and inclusion has been a key part of AT&T's success for more than a century — and it will continue to be integral to growing our business. We include diversity in everything we do from serving our customers in their native language to giving back to diverse communities with our education initiatives and ensuring our employee base reflects the communities in which we operate. We also have a proven record of commitment to supplier diversity, which includes being one of only 15 corporations that qualify as a member of the prestigious Billion Dollar Roundtable, an elite group of corporations that spends more than $1 billion annually with diverse companies."

Again, if the Church wants to truly create a culture that embraces diversity, it must put its money where its mouth is. This doesn't mean to the tune of one billion dollars; however, the church should allocate X amount dollars in the budget to help foster a culture of diversity. I recommend that every ministry have a diversity advocate within their organization. For larger organizations this could be a full-time role that has multiple responsibilities:

- reporting directly to the board and/or senior leader all things diversity
- developing a plan or strategy to be sensitive to issues of diversity in operations, culture, budget, community involvement, staffing, etc.
- identifying diversity strategy, goals, and objectives
- overall diversity advocating and planning

If the organization is not at the level of making this a full-time position, it should definitely be an added responsibility for a human resources professional, staff member, or volunteer within the organization that truly values diversity.

AT&T has demonstrated the ability to be a serious player and have almost unmatched success in the telecommunications world. Senior Vice President, Talent Development, and Chief Diversity Officer Cindy Brinkley talks about what contributes to AT&T's success. She stated, "We know that diverse, talented, and dedicated people are critical to AT&T's success. Investing in a well-educated diverse work force may be the single most important thing we can do to help America remain the leader in a digital, global economy. We're investing considerable time and resources today to develop tomorrow's leaders — with a committed eye toward ensuring those leaders bring different backgrounds, views, and experiences to their positions."

I have been to many, many, many church conferences where today's top ministry leaders impart leadership knowledge and wisdom into ministry leaders from around the globe. I have heard many ten-step programs on how to do XYZ and develop leaders in the Church; however, I have never heard one person share something as important and eloquent as Brinkley. If the Church wants to develop successful ministry leaders they should take the advice she gives above.

Assess → Believe → Change!

#1 Company for Diversity: Johnson and Johnson. More than any other company, Johnson & Johnson embodies ethical values. The company's employees base their decision making on the company credo, which emphasizes the importance of serving its customers, employees, communities, and stockholders fairly and equitably. Johnson & Johnson's rise on *DiversityInc*'s Top 50 list is indicative of its increased commitment to diversity and using diversity specifically as a competitive business advantage.

Diversity strengths: In all four areas measured on the *DiversityInc* survey, this company is outstanding. Chairman and CEO William C. Weldon received a perfect score for diversity commitment, including meeting regularly with employee resource groups and having the chief diversity officer as a direct report. Weldon has also held a senior position on a nonprofit board tied to a multicultural group as he served on the Sullivan Commission on Diversity in the Health Professions Work Force. More than 6 percent of the bonuses of his direct reports are tied to diversity results. In addition, Johnson & Johnson has a very diverse board of directors consisting of 9 percent black, 9 percent Asian, and 9 percent Latino.

In the corporate and organizational communications area, Johnson & Johnson is one of the strongest companies ever seen. It has excellent employee-resource groups, which are becoming even more valuable to the company under Vice President and Chief Diversity Officer Anthony Carter, and includes a group for employees of Middle Eastern and North African heritage. Even in these difficult economic times, the company's mission to serve its community remains very strong. This is emphasized by its supplier diversity, which includes sponsoring business-school programs for key diverse suppliers and sponsoring memberships and other professional development for diverse suppliers, such as its participation in the National Minority Manufacturing Institute.

Johnson & Johnson has been a household name as it relates to health care needs for longer than most of us can remember. They have a commitment to being the best, and that shows by the large number of companies they beat out to be number one on this list. If you check out Johnson & Johnson's website you'll see that their home page is the poster child for diversity.

The Church must stay focused on what's right and what it takes to be the best. What's right and what's best is creating a culture where everyone truly feels welcome to walk through a church's doors, be confronted with the gospel, and have the opportunity to enter into a personal relationship with Jesus.

I'll close with this quote from Chairman and CEO William Sheldon: "Diversity and inclusion are part of the fabric of our businesses and are vital to our future success worldwide. The principles of diversity and inclusion are rooted in our credo and enhance our ability to deliver products and services to advance the health and well-being of people throughout the world. *We cannot afford to reduce our focus on these critical areas in any business climate*" (emphasis added). The Church is dealing with issues of eternal life and eternal death and we cannot afford to reduce our focus on a critical issue like church diversity, especially in the 21st century.

Assess → Believe → Change!

 ## CHURCH DIVERSITY CHALLENGE 5

What are some corporate practices that you utilize in the leadership of your church? How effective have these practices been?

What are some of the corporate diversity practices listed in this chapter that stood out to you most? Why?

How do you think incorporating some of these corporate diversity practices would benefit your church?

What one or two corporate diversity practices could you see implementing within your own church? What next steps do you need to take in order to begin the implementation process?

Endnotes
1. Diversity Inc. information, survey data, and quotes cited in this chapter may be found at http://www.diversityinc.com/pages/DI_50.shtml?id=7617.
2. Bill Hybels, *Courageous Leadership* (Grand Rapids, MI: Zondervan, 2009).

6

Churches Ahead of the Curve: Small Stories Shaping the Big Picture

Fear is the prison where potential is confined.

— Scott Williams

Check out video 6
www.nlpg.com/churchdiversity

The fact that you have made it this far in this book is evidence that somewhere deep down inside you have a desire to be a part of this movement to change the heart and face of the Church. As we are nearing the end (I mean beginning) of our journey together, I thought it would be important to allow you to hear from some "Do the Right Thing" ministry leaders around the globe. These are guys that I have personally connected with, all great men of God with great hearts that embrace diversity. They are leaders who are ahead of the diversity curve, whereas the majority of churches and ministry leaders, especially in the United States, are behind the curve.

According to sociologist Dr. Michael Emerson in the *TIME* magazine article "Can Mega Churches Bridge the Racial Divide?"[1] only 7 percent of the churches in the United States are ahead of the curve. His research findings are that 93 percent of churches in the United States are racially segregated. This data, or curve as I'm referring to it, is based on a multiracial church being defined as a church where the predominant group is not larger than 80 percent. In other words, only 7 percent of churches in the United States have reached the 20 percent benchmark to be considered a multiracial or diverse church. But among evangelical churches with attendance of 1,000 people or more, the slice has more than quadrupled, from 6 percent in 1998 to 25 percent in 2007. Such rapid change in such big institutions "blows my mind," says Emerson. Some of the country's largest churches are involved: the very biggest, Joel Osteen's Lakewood Community Church in Houston (43,500 members), is split evenly among blacks, Hispanics, and a category containing whites and Asians. According to David Campbell, a political scientist at Notre Dame studying the trend, "If tens of millions of Americans start sharing faith across racial boundaries, it could be one of the final steps transcending race as our great divider."[2] Mega churches sometimes take a lot of flack, but it looks like they may be trending a little ahead of the curve on the issue of diversity in the Church.

I was able to ask each of the pastors featured in this chapter (most of whom lead mega-churches) a few questions relative to church diversity in order for us to learn from their perspectives. There are a growing number of pastors that could be featured in this section; however, the ones featured in this section are men of God that I have met, know personally, and firmly believe that you should hear from. This group of leaders and their ministries are diverse, their stories are different, their perspectives are unique, and yet their hearts have a unified beat. I will let their stories speak for themselves and provide my "key thoughts" at the conclusion of each pastor's section. One important aspect of these pastors' leadership I want to point out is that they are courageous. They have overcome the fear of the scary proposition and huge commitment of church diversity. Something I like to say about fear is a phrase that I came up with when I was a prison warden: "Fear is the prison where potential is confined." God has not given us the spirit of fear. Stop being scared and be a part of moving the Church from where it is to where it needs to be. Each and every one of our small stories will help to shape the BIG church diversity picture.

Believe It — Preach It — Live It

Herbert's Story

Pastor Herbert Cooper, People's Church, Oklahoma City, Oklahoma

People are oftentimes scared, intimidated, and fearful of differences, so we tend to stay away from people and environments that are different from what we are used to.

— Herbert Cooper

The grand opening of People's Church was on May 12, 2002, with 65 people in attendance. In the beginning, our church met in a movie theater of a local shopping mall. In August 2004, People's Church purchased 50 acres and built two facilities over a three-year period. Over the last eight years, the church has grown to 4,000 people in weekend attendance. More importantly, every single weekend we are seeing people give their lives to Christ. People's Church is all about more changed lives.

My heart for diversity goes back to an early age. I grew up interacting with people from other cultures and nationalities and have always had close friends who were different races than me. After college, I married a white lady, and I'm straight up hood rat African American (just playing about the hood rat!). Since my wife and I got married, we have had a burden and passion to see the church diversified and unified at the same time.

Diversity is important to me because it's important to God. Jesus desires for the Church to be one, according to the Book of John. Jesus did not say that people would know that we are His disciples because we have a super large church, or because we have millions of dollars in our budget, or because we have hundreds of thousands of square feet of plush facility. He said the world will know we are His disciples because we love one another. I take that literally. Black, white, red, or yellow; we ought to love one another. We ought to get along. We ought to care about each other. We ought to be able to interact and love each other deeply. I also firmly believe that we are stronger together than we are apart. I truly believe that our differences and weaknesses, when put together, make a stronger church and Body of Christ. For example, my wife and I are total opposites in many ways, but together we are stronger and make a dynamite team. The Church is the same way. We are better together. We are stronger together. We will accomplish more together.

Creating a Culture of Diversity

When we began our church, it was interesting watching different races of people who had never been around another race interact with each other. There were definitely some major uncomfortable and awkward moments. There was one particular couple in our church that had both grown up in upper middle class white families in Mississippi. They had recently moved to Oklahoma City and started attending People's Church. This couple grew up learning and thinking negatively toward black people. Now they had a black pastor, and they decided to join one of our small groups led by a black couple that met in a house located in a predominantly black neighborhood. This couple personally told me that they had no idea how racist they were, and God used People's Church and that small group to strip away all the junk from their hearts. I think one of the most interesting things about watching this couple and other people who have interacted with different cultures is that after a while they come to the conclusion that we're all basically alike. We all deal with the same junk and sin.

All of us experience the same pains, hurts, struggles, fears, and temptations. Don't get me wrong, this hood rat likes chitterlings, hog malls, and collard greens, but besides that, we all have the same needs. We all bleed red and we have all sinned and fallen short of God's glory. We all need Jesus. We all need His love, forgiveness, mercy, grace, and hope!

One of the biggest challenges in creating a diverse culture is getting people to connect with others. Convincing them and teaching them to connect in small group settings can be a struggle. However, our biggest win is when people do connect, and we get to see guards go down, hearts open wide, and life change happen because people got together and God did what only He can do.

Confront the Elephant in the Pew

I think people are unwilling to confront church diversity because most of us are used to being around people like ourselves. As a result, we get comfortable with people like ourselves and uncomfortable with people who don't look like us. People are oftentimes scared, intimidated, and fearful of differences, so we tend to stay away from people and environments that are different from what we are used to. When we stay away from other races and environments, we tend to struggle with stereotyping other races and cultures because of our lack of knowledge.

I think another reason churches don't confront the issue is because there is still a presence of racism. This happens in black, white, Indian, Hispanic, Chinese, and Japanese churches. Racism is even found in the pulpit. It's a heart issue and a sin issue when our hearts are filled with bigotry, hatred, or the elitism mentality, which thinks, "I'm better than you" because of the color of my skin or where I live.

Another reason churches don't confront the issue is because it can get messy. It can be messy once you start mixing cultures, because when you start having diversity you start confronting issues of the heart. It can be messy to invite other cultures and races to your church because your church might start having worshipers who are Republican, Democrat, or Independent and view things differently from you. It can be messy when little yellow-skin Tim starts dating little brown-skin Tina. It can be messy navigating through incorporating rock, gospel, rap, or country music into the Sunday morning worship experience to connect with everybody in the church. Consequently, it's easier for some churches to stay the way they are so they can avoid dealing with the mess that might be created from having a diverse church.

Be Intentional

We teach diversity and unity from the platform. We are very intentional about who is on the platform. We realize that people want to see themselves represented on the platform. We also model it in our staff, as we have been diverse since day one. Our original staff consisted of our worship leader (a white man), who is now our executive director of creative arts, and me. Our board has always been diverse. It's important that people see themselves represented on the platform and in the leadership of the church.

Pastor Herbert's Final Advice

Preach it! The most powerful tool of any pastor is the pulpit on Sunday morning. You always get what you preach. If you want people to serve, you preach on serving. If you want people to live holy, you preach on holiness. If you want people to give, you preach on giving. If you want a diverse church, start preaching and teaching on why it's important to God and to you.

You must be intentional about making the staff, leadership, and platform diverse. Also, the pastors and leaders of the church need to model diversity to the church by having friends from other races and cultures. It's hard to teach a church to embrace diversity if you're not willing to do it yourself. You have to live it and not just teach it.

My Key Thoughts on Herbert's Story

- Church diversity is born out of a burden and passion to see the Church diversified.
- Diversity should be important to us, because it's important to God.
- People are often scared of and intimidated by differences.
- Don't be naive; racism is real and exists in the Church.
- Believe it — preach it — live it!

Lives and Dinner Tables Diversified

JB's Story

Pastor John Bryson, Fellowship Memphis, Memphis, Tennessee

You go to war for diversity and you win the secondary battles against preference and consumerism as a bonus.

— John Bryson

Tennessee

Memphis

I believe from Genesis 1:1 to Revelation 22:21, God's heart is "all nations." The early church in Acts was a multicultural, multiracial, inter-generational body of believers. Racism raised its head in Acts 10 when Peter would no longer eat with Gentiles. Paul calls him out in Galatians 2 by saying that racial division was "not in line with the gospel" (Gal. 2:14). In our racialized country and racialized world, race and diversity are gospel issues.

The Book of Revelation describes some scenes of heaven. The scenes include meals and worship conducted with every "tongue, tribe, nation, and people group" (Rev. 5:9). I often tell people if they do not like a diverse church, they will hate heaven. Diverse corporate meals, worship, and life is where we are headed . . . for eternity.

Fellowship Memphis had a dream to see a church emerge that looked like the city where it was birthed. We begged God to unleash the gospel in such a way that normal cultural divides like race, age, education, and socio-economic class would be obliterated by the gospel. Our goal was not just a diverse gathering for an hour and a half on Sundays (our NBA team the Grizzlies had already accomplished that). Our goal was to see people's dinner tables and lives diversified. By God's grace, we are seeing people from all walks of life experiencing the power of a diverse community.

Creating a Culture of Diversity

To go to battle for a diverse church, for most, you are going to war with idolatry. Many of us have race and culture, not the gospel, as a primary identifier of who we are. You are also going to war with preference. Many of us have approached church as a consumer looking for our preferences.

Rather than laying down our rights for the sake of the whole, we hold on to our rights because they are comfortable. To embrace diversity, one must lay down one's rights. The Church must unapologetically create a theology of discomfort.

I believe in that Revelation moment we will all experience in the future, when every tongue, tribe, nation, and people group are worshiping God together. I don't think we are going to care if we are singing a Donnie McClurkin song, a Chris Tomlin song, or a Charles Wesley song. I don't think we are going to care if what accompanies us is an organ, a guitar, an orchestra, a keyboard, the spoons, or a jug. Why? Because the object of our worship so consumes us that the means through which we work becomes an appropriate lesser issue. We are so far from that in the modern Church; we split churches over those "lesser" issues.

You go to war for diversity and you win the secondary battles against preference and consumerism as a bonus.

Confront the Elephant in the Pew

We will truly begin to confront the elephant when unleashing the gospel has dominated our hearts, our view of other people (specifically those who are racially and culturally different from us), and our view of church. We don't deal with the elephant because we worship comfort, ease, preference, and predictability.

As a white dude from a majority culture perspective, we don't deal with the elephant in the pew because we don't have to. We live in an incredibly racialized culture and most white folks are oblivious to that reality and painfully ignorant on issues of race. The Church in general is embarrassingly ignorant on race, and much less does it have a biblical theology of race. Most pastors I know can talk to me on a PhD level on issues of theology until I bring up race and diversity. Then it feels like we engage in a third grade level discussion. It's sad.

Be Intentional

We are intentional about everything. Literally, every decision is run through the diversity priority and grid.

Pastor JB's Final Advice

One intentional move we made beyond just having a diverse staff was to ask Bryan Loritts to take the mantle of lead pastor from within our leadership team and preach a majority of the time. Bryan is a phenomenal leader and preacher. With a majority culture in our church at the time, we felt like it would be significant for Bryan (who happens to be black) to function in the lead pastor role and be the most consistent presence in our pulpit.

We also felt the value of diversity had to come from an authentic place within all our leadership and membership, and that it would show itself in many more arenas than just our church and what our Sunday crowd looks like. We look for leaders — from elders to staff to leaders within our body — who live out our values, including diversity, in how they do life, who is around their dinner table, and the choices they make day-to-day and week-to-week.

My Key Thoughts on JB's Story

- If you don't like a diverse church, you will hate heaven.
- Be a part of this church diversity movement and war for diversity and you win the secondary battles against preference and consumerism as a bonus.
- The Church won't confront the elephant because we worship comfort, ease, preference, and predictability. The majority culture won't confront it because they don't have to.
- Most pastors can have a PhD level conversation about theology but are ignorant about issues of race in the Church.
- The Church must unapologetically create a theology of discomfort.

It's a Result of the Gospel

Derwin's Story

Pastor Derwin Gray, Transformation Church, Charlotte, North Carolina

> *Multi-ethnic church is not in addition to the gospel, it is as a result of the gospel.*
> — Derwin Gray

The genesis of Transformation Church (TC) was birthed in my heart over a two-year process while taking classes at Southern Evangelical Seminary in Charlotte, North Carolina, under Dr. Barry Leventhal. As I read through the New Testament, God wrote a new passion in my heart, a love for "the Church" and her role in transforming the world. It was as if I had a conversion experience; to quote Bill Hybels, I realized that "the hope of the world is the Church!"

As an itinerant preacher, I noticed early in ministry that no matter what part of the country I was preaching in, the churches, conferences, and events were racially segregated. I could not understand how just about every facet of American society was integrated, from corporate America to public schools and sports teams, yet the Church was not. I knew this wall of segregation was shattering God's heart and was a poor witness to those who don't follow Christ. For years I was critical about this issue. But God challenged me: don't criticize — create!

I didn't want to create! It's so much easier to criticize! The final nudge that pushed me over the edge took place while I was attending a conference at Willow Creek in the fall of 2005. While lounging in the Willow Creek bookstore, an African American pastor from Michigan began to talk with me. It was small talk at first. Then, out of nowhere, this pastor asked, "Are you a pastor?"

I said, "No," and communicated that I had no plans of ever being one either. The pastor fired back, "God has a call on your life; I can hear it in your voice. You're a pastor and many will follow your leadership because you're following Christ. By the end 2006, you will be a pastor." I was thinking, *Okay. I'm done now. See ya later.*

About an hour later I found myself in Willow Creek's massive auditorium, lost in the worship songs before the next communicator was to present. With hands raised high and my affections toward God, I heard a voice say, "By the end of 2006, you will be a pastor." My soul was arrested and I sprinted out of the auditorium and immediately called my wife, Vicki, and said, "Sweetheart, I think God is calling us to pastor a church." There was dead silence on the phone. Vicki wanted to be part of pastoring a church about as much as she wanted to swim across shark-infested waters. Over the next few months, as we prayed and sought God together, we both became convinced of God's calling. And before the end of 2006, I became a pastor.

In 2007 I helped plant a church in Charlotte, North Carolina. After three years of co-leading this church plant, following God's call on my life and my desire to plant "a multiethnic, multigenerational, mission-shaped community that loves God completely (upward), ourselves correctly (inward), and our neighbors compassionately (outward)," we founded and planted Transformation Church on Super Bowl Sunday, February 7, 2010, with a multiethnic group of gifted servant-leaders that we affectionately call the "Dream Team."

Eight months after the launch, God has grown Transformation Church from 178 people to a multiethnic, multigenerational, mission-shaped community of over 1,300, where 200 people have committed their lives to Jesus and His kingdom since the church's birth.

Creating a Culture of Diversity

The first ingredient to building a healthy multiethnic church is that the leaders' hearts must be seized by the biblical conviction that God wants His Church to be multiethnic, *whenever possible*. Multiethnic church is not in addition to the gospel; it is as a *result* of the gospel. We are not only reconciled to our tri-personal God, but we are reconciled to one another across cultural, socioeconomic, and ethnic barriers. Jesus ripped down the dividing wall through His sinless life, substitutionary death on the Cross, and His glorious Resurrection (Eph. 2:11–18, 3:6; Rev. 7:9; Gal. 3:28).

Second, pray and fast for a leadership team that reflects the multiethnic diversity of the community in which God has placed you to be a missionary outpost (local church). I knew that if I wanted Transformation Church to be a multiethnic congregation, I needed my staff to reflect the multiethnic diversity that I wanted the congregation to embody.

Third, diversity in worship styles is crucial to developing a healthy multiethnic church. Some weekends our worship style will reflect a passion rock sound, another weekend it will reflect an R & B sound or Latino sound. And some weekends you may hear rock, R & B, and Latino, along with an ancient hymn, in the same worship service.

I prayed for and recruited a gifted black worship leader named Jasper Hall who grew up in the "black church" but spent his adult life singing in the "white church." Jasper brings a rich understanding of multiethnic worship to Transformation Church. Having a worship leader who values musical diversity will help in cultivating an ethnically diverse church. Our diverse musical worship styles have created a culture of celebration and servanthood. Diverse musical worship styles kick consumerism in its face!

Fourth, partner with the Holy Spirit in creating a multiethnic ethos. How do we do that? As the lead pastor, I must continually cast a God-sized, beautiful, compelling vision and teach from the sacred Scriptures that the outworking of the gospel produces a multiethnic, mission-shaped church. The gospel not only transforms us personally, it also transforms how we see and interact with people of diverse ethnic and socio-economic backgrounds.

Confront the Elephant in the Pew

There are several elephants we need to confront when we talk about diversity in the Church. First, the recent American Church is a child of Dr. Donald McGavran's so-called homogeneous unity principle. This ministry model teaches that people like to become Christ followers without crossing racial (ethnic), linguistic, or class barriers. Many church leaders, knowingly and unknowingly, hold to this ministry model.

Second, success begets imitation. The majority of hereos in the evangelical stream of the faith lead homogeneous mega-churches. And their disciples who attend their conferences and read their books follow their heroes' homogeneous ministry models, which produces more homogeneous churches, even though their churches are located in ethnically diverse communities.

In essence, our successful heroes do not pastor multiethnic mega churches. And why should they? In this ministry model, success is determined by what pragmatically works (big building, big budgets, and lots of butts in seats) instead of biblical and theological reflection.

Third, we have an underdeveloped view of the gospel. The gospel reconciles us to God and to one another. The early Church outside of Jerusalem was a multiethnic church. Jews who once considered Gentiles as unclean found themselves worshiping, praying, doing life, and being on missions together because Jesus tore down the barriers and made a new people (Eph. 2:11–22; 3:1-13; Book of Galatians).

Fourth, a lack of intentionality. If we are unintentional about building a multiethnic church, we will be intentional about not building a multiethnic church. If my staff was all black, and if our music was all Gospel and R & B, and if our ministry leaders were all black, what message would I be sending non-black people? My words may say "non-blacks are welcome," but my actions and ministry model would not. If we do not build deep, meaningful relationships with people of different ethnic backgrounds, it will be difficult to build a multiethnic staff. Before we can build a multiethnic church, we must live a multiethnic life.

Fifth, we do not know how to build multiethnic churches. Our heroes pastor homogeneous churches. We have little to no example. In seminary, I was not taught how to build a multi-ethnic church. It wasn't even mentioned. The list of multiethnic church practioners is a short list. I had to search hard to find and connect with multi-ethnic church pioneers.

The sixth challenge is fear. We fear what we do not understand. Our fear is similar to Peter's fear in Acts chapter 10. Peter had not interacted with the Gentiles, so when God told him to go take the gospel to a Gentile, he was reluctant and fearful. God was calling him to new a ministry, yet he wanted to walk in the well-established ruts of the past.

Likewise, in creating a multiethnic church, the homogeneous church leadership experiences fear. The biggest fear is the releasing of power. The homogeneous leadership must ask the question, "Will I let the non-dominant culture have roles of leadership and power to influence the culture of the church?" This is scary. But it is so worth it!

Be Intentional

An example of creating a multiethnic ethos is the practice of accommodation instead of assimilation. To accommodate people means that we welcome people and their ethnic/cultural/socio-economic diversity into the life of the Transformation Church by creating pathways for them to express their diversity in the life of the church. To assimilate people means that you want people who are different ethnically, culturally, and socio-economically to leave their differences in the parking lot.

We are also prayerful and strategic about our ministries (kids, teens, etc.) at Transformation Church having ethnically diverse leadership and participation.

The biggest challenge is church leadership in America. It can be discouraging because it appears that many leaders in the Church in America are content with homogeneous, segregated churches. Recently, at a national church planting meeting, I asked if multiethnic church planting was a part of their vision. My question was at first ignored. Then I was verbally attacked when I made a biblical and theological case that we do not have the right to plant churches in ethnically diverse communities and not be intentional about reflecting the diversity in that community through staffing and ministry philosophy.

A pastor I greatly respect told me that if he tried to transition his church to become multiethnic, many of the men in his congregation would be afraid their daughters would marry a black or Latino man so he was resistant to trying to be multiethnic.

A pastor of a first-generation Latino congregation said that he does not want to be multiethnic because the second-generation Latinos would lose their Latino ethnic identity. I've also had various first-generation Asian Christ-followers tell me the same thing.

Another challenge or disappointment has been Christ-followers who have told us they will not stay and plug into Transformation Church because our multiethnic diversity is a problem for them. The vestiges of racism are still alive and well.

There are signs of hope. Sociologist Dr. Michael Emerson found, "The number of diverse evangelical churches of 1,000 members or more has grown from 6 percent in 1998 to more than 25 percent."

Pastor Derwin's Final Advice

My advice is this: do not give up on seeing the Church becoming multiethnic! God is doing a new thing and using people like you, who desire to see the

Church on earth embody this beautiful picture: "After this I looked, and behold, a great multitude that no one could number, from every nation, from all tribes and peoples and languages, standing before the throne and before the Lamb" (Rev. 7:9; ESV).

My Key Thoughts on Derwin's Story

- Multiethnic church is not in addition to the gospel, it is as a *result* of the gospel.
- Diverse musical worship styles kick consumerism in its face!
- Before we can build a multiethnic church, we must live a multiethnic life.
- Church diversity must be embraced by seminaries and church planting organizations.
- We fear what we don't understand.

Racism and Tribalism

Femi's Story

Pastor Femi Monehin God's Favourite House, Lagos, Nigeria

If the leadership is racist/tribalistic, there will be no executive willing to Confront the Elephant in the Pew.

— Femi Monehin

I'm Femi Monehin, privileged to pastor God's Favourite House, a fast-growing church in Lagos, Nigeria. It's easy to think that an all-black nation will not have issues of segregation. To the contrary, Nigeria, being the most populous black nation in the world, has over 250 *distinct* tribes, each with its own language and culture. However, only three are mainly recognized politically: Yoruba, Igbo, and Hausa. The tribalism can be so deep that listing Yoruba before Igbo and Hausa can be an issue of contention. Sadly, this mentality has crept into the Church. I vividly remember a time when my wife and I hosted our key leaders at our home. During the gathering, two of our guys were playing a competitive Nintendo Wii boxing game. We heard one of the wives say these words to her husband, "Don't allow this Yoruba man to beat you!" I felt so pained from what I heard and what I felt. Ever since that day, we have been very intentional in creating an

atmosphere of diversity and inclusion in our worship and all aspects of doing life together.

Creating a Culture of Diversity

Music and rhythm is very crucial in our culture — so we are very intentional and deliberately weave songs from various tribal languages into our worship experiences. It's amazing to see how people easily connect seeing other people not from their tribe, worshiping God in their dialect. It creates an atmosphere of unity. A major challenge is the suspicion that arose from the civil war and the Western interference and the "divide and rule" post-colonial political structure. However, when people from all over the country are able to rise to a level in church leadership without any acrimony, it speaks volumes and unites. I remember an elderly lady (a mother of one of our former leaders, from a different part of the country) saying these words, "My son and his wife are pastors in a *strange land*! Praise God!"

Confront the Elephant in the Pew

In my opinion, there are three reasons why people are unwilling to confront the elephant in the pew.

1. They are tribalistic/racist. For some strange reason, some people see themselves as superior just because they are from a particular race or tribe. A lot of this discrimination has been wired into them by uninformed parenting. When you have such people as church leaders, they attract like-minded people (whether they are concious of it or not). If the leadership is racist/tribalistic, there will be no executive willing to confront the elephant in the pew.
2. They are not tribalistic/racist themselves but are afraid of other people's opinions. In Galatians 2:11–13 Peter didn't discriminate until he saw other "tribalistic" Jews. Leaders have to influence culture and not the other way round.
3. They sincerely have no clue. Some leaders are clueless about this reality.

Be Intentional

At God's Favourite House, we are intentional about breaking down tribalistic/racist barriers.

First, we deliberately cast vision on our culture of diversity. The social scars that a lot of people bear makes it imperative for us to deliberately communicate our culture of diversity. Some people tend to be suspicious of otherwise harmless gestures of others who are not of the same tribe. If not dealt with from the top, these "little leaven" can leaven the whole lump. What is leaven? In the old days, when people made bread, they included an ingredient called leaven. Leaven is a yeast that makes bread rise. It creates air pockets in the dough, which end up being the tiny holes of air in finished bread. Have you ever had bread that had air pockets in one end of the loaf, and none in the other? Jesus compares this to sin and hypocrisy in our lives and ministries — it can ruin the whole thing. In 1 Corinthians 5:6–7 it talks about leaven: "Your boasting is not good. Don't you know that a little yeast leavens the whole batch of dough? Get rid of the old yeast, so that you may be a new unleavened batch — as you really are."

Second, we bring diversity through our music. We deliberately choose songs and styles from different cultures. Whether we like it or not, certain cultures are "tilted" toward certain styles of music. I really believe that music is a very powerful unifying tool. We appreciate our diversity and it makes a fellowship truly colorful.

Finally, we are intentional in our leadership development. We don't discriminate in who leads any aspect of our ministry. Everyone is able to develop and exercise his or her God-given gifts without the inhibition of segregation.

Pastor Femi's Final Advice

It's important as ministry leaders and the Body of Christ that we be deliberate about issues of diversity in the Church. The reality for the Church is that nothing significant happens by chance. The change that we need to see will come as a result of deliberately casting vision for diversity. We must carry our deliberate and intentional efforts over into all of our ministry areas including our worship and music. Our worship team should deploy musical styles that truly cut across cultures.

Everything rises and falls with leadership. Leaders should be inclusive about the players that are represented on the leadership team. Leadership decisions should also be deliberate if we want to see church diversity become a reality.

My Key Thoughts on Femi's Story

- Racism and tribalism are prevalent in the Church around the globe — even in nations perceived as being one race or one culture.
- Music is a globally powerful and unifying tool.
- Ministry leaders can be consciously or subconsciously clueless to the realities of church diversity.

- Social and racial injustices still have an impact on minority culture; therefore, fostering "separate but equal" church mentality.
- Nothing significant happens by chance — be deliberate!

From Brokenness to Wholeness

Bruce's Story

Pastor Bruce Reyes-Chow, Mission Bay Community Church, San Francisco, California

Ultimately we will not be able to fully embrace the diversity of church life and the many manifestations of the larger church family until we can each claim our part in the brokenness that exists when it comes to issues of race.

— Bruce Reyes-Chow

The congregation that I serve is a small church in San Francisco. We fit a particular niche of being theologically and socially progressive, Christ-centered, young, and ethnically diverse. We look much like San Francisco: a mix of mostly Asian Americans and white folks with a smaller percentage of African Americans and Latina/os. Our community is made up of mostly millenials, for whom issues of race and diversity look very different from those of previous generations. We have done a pretty good job of not thinking we are "beyond" race in any way, but live with the understanding that race can bring complexity and diversity to the community.

Creating a Culture of Diversity

The biggest challenge is that people do not understand that talking about race is complex and is not simply something that we can sit down and "solve." There is, for many, an unspoken feeling that diversity is a problem that must be organized into a safe, manageable reality rather than a gift from God that must be deftly navigated in order to fully experience the wonder that is creation, *and* that truly living diversity is ongoing and ever-changing. If I had to choose one struggle, it would be around the issues of "color-blindness" that many well-meaning people have. The "I don't see you as [insert ethnic group here]" perspective, while noble, does two things that are not helpful. One, it assumes that one's race is something that the person *wants* someone else to get beyond and, two, too often the "beyond" that we are striving for is simply a generic "white" culture that, in the end, perpetuates a "lesser than" understanding of people of color. In terms of "wins," simply being able to be the pastor of a multiethnic congregation where being Asian American can be part of my story, but does not confine or define me in totality, is a lovely place to be. The congregation's ability to see me as a complex person as I pastor them only shows that we have been able to create a context where we do not avoid complexity, but we embrace and live it.

Confront the Elephant in the Pew

The easy answer to why people are unwilling to confront the elephant in the pew is the fact that it is easier if we just avoid any conversations that have the potential to create tension, conflict, or social awkwardness. If we can just make it through our particular interactions without conflict, then we will be okay, and we can make the claim that issues of "race" do not exist in our church. As we know, in all relationships conflict avoidance does more harm than good. I believe that the biggest part of the avoidance has to deal with each of us failing to own our roles in the ongoing struggles about race. We are afraid of sounding dumb, saying the wrong thing, or admitting privilege while others are still figuring out how to embrace the complexities of their own cultural lives. Ultimately, we will not be able to fully embrace the diversity of church life and the many manifestations of the larger church family until we can each claim our part in the brokenness that exists when it comes to issues of race. It is only when we talk and claim brokenness that we will have the ability to embrace and live wholeness.

Be Intentional

I talk about my ethnic background, not as a platform for issues, but as a simple part of my life. The congregation knows about my Asian American background (Chinese and Filipino) and how that has informed my understanding of my faith and life — from what I feel about politics to how I raise my kids. This does not take anything away from being able to pastor non-Asians but models a way for us all to be whole people, diverse in our individuality but whole in our communal relationships.

When we take the position of "I don't see color," then we no longer have to acknowledge the realities of our own prejudice and privilege as well as the real experiences of others. We stifle conversations that must happen around race in the United States and squelch the possibilities of discovering together that one of the greatest gifts of U.S. culture and the world is our diverse racial and ethnic backgrounds. Be intentional!

Pastor Bruce's Final Advice

The biggest problem I see with churches that want to be multicultural is that they too often set as a goal a particular look or setting to measure success. Any true multicultural church community is open to embracing the diversity around them. We must keep talking about race and how we engage the conversation because how we live impacts the ability for people of color to fully live as God intends.

The lack of intentionality and inadvertent decisions can affect how people view themselves when they walk through the doors of the church. No person wants to be seen as "the brown family" that helps to make a community diverse. I don't think that people are intentionally doing this, but unless that family or person is loved, pastored, and understood as a family that happens to be brown, that will be how attention is perceived. Multiculturalism is complex and not always about race, but also age, gender, class, and church experience. Seeing any one person as solely one of these things will doom any multicultural community to living a shallow experience of community that does not deepen our understanding of God's beautiful and complex creation.

My Key Thoughts on Bruce's Story

- Don't embrace the argument of "I don't see color."
- Our race helps form our understanding of our faith and life — from what we feel about politics, race, and culture, to how we raise our kids.
- Although ethnicity is a part of each of our life stories, it doesn't have to confine or limit our thinking.
- Issues of race are complex and they are not something that we just sit down and solve. It takes time.
- There are no dumb questions. . . . We must begin to ask the tough questions and begin the necessary discussions to address the issues of church diversity.

Multiethnic in the Midst of Lily White

Jerry's Story

Pastor Jerry McQuay, Christian Life Center, Tinley Park, Illinois

*I just don't see how anyone can believe that lost
people matter to God and not embrace diversity.*

— Jerry McQuay

We started Christian Life Center in 1990, with intentional
efforts to be a multicultural church from day one. We included
African American communities in our telemarketing and mar-
keting efforts. We openly addressed diversity and a heart for
embracing church diversity in the opening message. We also
included African Americans and minorities on stage during our
inaugural service.

Stereotypically, I'm probably the "least likely" individual to
champion diversity, especially in the Church, given my upbringing
in the deep South — which included only all-white churches, camps, and Bible
school experiences. Yet there seems to be a "grace" upon our ministry that has
included significant results from itinerant preaching, bus ministry efforts in an
all-white church where we served on staff, and leading the first church we pastored from its all-white roots to about 25 percent black membership in five
years. The reality is that I just don't see how anyone can believe that lost people
matter to God and not embrace diversity.

Creating a Culture of Diversity

Our biggest challenge in the early days was opposition and resentment
from the white nucleus that helped us start the church. I simply outlasted them,
and eventually those who were opposed left the church.

For the first half of our church's history, the racial balance was terrific —
about 45 percent white, 45 percent black, and about 10 percent Hispanic or
Asian. But when we outgrew our small auditorium and built a larger facility, we
doubled in size in about two years. The growth was fueled almost entirely by
the African American segment of our congregation. I've told my friends that if
we won a new black family this Sunday, by next weekend they would have
invited their aunts, uncles, cousins, and friends, and they would also be visiting
the church. On the other hand, if we won a new white family this Sunday, it

might take about six months before they'd even tell someone where they attended church.

That cultural reality has brought us a new challenge — because as people of color became the *majority* of our congregation, some of our white members became uncomfortable. I don't think the ministry changed: worship and teaching and all of that remained the same, but the reality is that whites have never been in a minority position in our country, and just from a sociological standpoint, we don't know how to handle it. In more recent years, as the black segment of our congregation has grown exponentially, our challenge has been to maintain diversity. As the church became predominantly black, many of our white congregants became uncomfortable. Being a minority for most of our white congregants was totally new and many were admittedly uncomfortable in a minority position. We've experienced some signs of "white flight," particularly from members whose children reach dating age.

No matter the challenges, our biggest win is simply that we have built a multicultural church in a community that is virtually lily white in the suburbs of Chicago.

Confront the Elephant in the Pew

The plain and simple reason that people are unwilling to confront the elephant in the pew is that it's uncomfortable. Few people have really had genuine relationships of diversity; therefore, all we know are stereotypical thoughts, impressions, and comments of people who look different than we do, as we remain with "our own kind." Confronting this issue publicly creates tension, and most of us don't like that feeling — although I've found the benefits extend to every group. There are definite benefits from the tension diversity conversations and decisions create.

Be Intentional

We have been intentional in all areas and it pretty much has been the same things we emphasized from the beginning:

- ensuring that our stage represented diversity
- being intentional about visual announcements and media — ensuring they reflected diversity
- challenging each ministry (youth, worship, children, small groups, etc.) to be sure that diversity was reflected in leadership
- making sure diversity was reflected in our governing boards

- inviting guest speakers who represent the racial diversity of the congregation
- honoring some traditions from different cultures and races. We do a New Year's Eve "watch" service that is big in the African American community and we also offer Christmas Eve services that are big in the white community. I usually make a point of encouraging our members to try both — not just the one that appeals to them.

Pastor Jerry's Final Advice

Intentionality. Intentionality. Intentionality. It will never happen by accident. Be willing to accept the tension that comes with the decision to pursue multiculturalism.

In addition, because I've seen the "grace" that's on us, which is the obvious difference between friends who've sincerely tried to become multicultural without success — I've got to believe that this is a God thing. So I would strongly encourage anyone who wants to create this culture to pray for God's favor on their efforts, and to "listen" for His directives.

My Key Thoughts on Jerry's Story

- Intentionality and a heart for diversity from the beginning is key.
- You can't believe that lost people matter to God and not embrace diversity.
- If you don't have genuine relationships of diversity, you settle for stereotypes.
- As one ethnic segment grows, a church must be equally as intentional to maintain diversity.
- A multi-ethnic church can exist in a virtually lily-white suburb.

From Little Rock to Hollywood

Philip's Story

**Pastor Philip Wagner, Oasis Church,
Los Angeles-Hollywood, California**

*My hope is that one day when churches are asked how
they achieve racial diversity it will be like asking a fish
how it swims. I'm not really sure it just comes naturally.*

— Philip Wagner

Living in the heart of Los Angeles — Hollywood — our city is a melting pot of diversity. People of all colors, backgrounds, and nationalities live here in Los Angeles; and yet, unfortunately, most churches do not reflect the racial diversity of our city. In fact, most churches in America lack racial diversity. The Oasis Church has always had racial diversity. It is one of the unique things about our church. From the first day we started Oasis, there has been a diverse racial mix: black, brown, and white — Latino, European, Russian, Filipino, or African. It's amazing. I've always felt it was something God was doing and we just tried to not mess it up.

In our latest survey, our church's ethnic breakdown was 30 percent African American, 28 percent Caucasian, 15 percent Hispanic/Latino, 14 percent Asian, and 13 percent multiracial and other diversities.

Creating a Culture of Diversity

My hope is that one day when churches are asked how they achieve racial diversity it will be like asking a fish how it swims: "I'm not really sure; it just comes naturally." But for now, that is just a dream. I believe in that dream. With God, all things are possible.

What's funny is the fact that God has even used me in this way. I was born in Little Rock, Arkansas. It was a racially segregated world. In 1957 I saw the integration of Central High School accompanied by the National Guard, which was covered by international news.

I was raised in a family with Southern roots and honestly, they were prejudiced. I had every reason and excuse to grow up with a racist attitude. Yet I didn't. None of us should blame our current attitude and perspective on our family upbringing or heritage. Whether it's racism or genuine acceptance and value of all human beings, it's a choice we all make in our own heart. God is using a white boy from Arkansas to lead a multiracial church in the heart of Hollywood — I love it.

Confront the Elephant in the Pew

The New Testament reveals that the work of Jesus Christ makes us all one: "There is neither Jew nor Gentile, neither slave nor free, nor is there male and female, for you are all one in Christ Jesus" (Gal. 3:28).

Many people are attracted to a multiracial congregation. It's often one of the first things people notice about our church. But in my 26 years of pastoring, I've learned that some people don't seem to have the capacity to "live" in that environment because they bring their own baggage, bias, hurts, and prejudices with them. Eventually they leave or they reveal their racially motivated frustrations.

It's easy to have a multiracial "audience" — go to any baseball game. It's a different issue to have a multiracial "community." Some are overly sensitive. Some are too insensitive. Others just flat out don't trust other races.

Being a white pastor, I remember the surprise and disappointment that I felt when I first heard that one of my African American friends and church members took a lot of heat from their family and friends for going to our church. They would often be asked, "Why would you go to a church where the pastor is white?" The pressure was on them to only support a leader that was their color.

I would hope that people, regardless of the race of the leader, would look primarily at the leader's heart, message, and friends . . . you know, "the content of their character not color of their skin." It's the love of God that allows people to accept, honor, and value one another even though we have different experiences, upbringing, and views.

Be Intentional

For some churches, achieving racial diversity will be natural; for others, it will have to be intentional, because they are overcoming years of distorted values, relationship "norms," deep wounds, or social stigmas. When I am asked by other pastors or leaders how they can get more diversity in their church, my answer is in the form of questions. These are questions you need to honestly ask yourself.

1. Who are your friends? Who do you hang out with? Who do you enjoy being with? When you invite people over to your house — do they all look like you? Are you comfortable with people of a different color of skin?

   If the pastor does not build friendships with people of other races, I doubt that diversity will be a significant part of the church. I often challenge people to ask, not "Am I prejudiced?" but "How prejudiced am I?" If we are honest, I think we all have some preconceived ideas of others.

2. Who is on your church team? Do you have a diverse mix of people on your leadership team? I don't suggest you just go out and pick random

people to be part of your leadership because of the color of their skin. But you may need to begin to bring in good solid leaders who are of diverse races for your leadership team to help build the value of diversity in your church congregation. This should really be an extension of your natural relationships.

3. Who do you value? Who are your heroes? I quote men and women of all races in my sermons. I tell stories in my messages using all races of people who are examples of faith or integrity. I hold them up as examples that should be followed.

   Some of my favorite leaders, musical artists, or actors are of diverse racial backgrounds and I admire them. It's just a natural expression for me. We mention often how we value the racial diversity that we see in our congregation. We thank God for it. We consider our diversity a special blessing and we pray for God's continual blessing in this area.

Even if you have a church with a small percentage of diversity, it would be great to pray and publically thank God for the percentage you do have and ask for more growth in that area. You may want to talk about how important it is that your church be an example in the community — especially in the area of diversity, and pray from the platform for God's guidance and grace in this area. As a congregation, we pray for racial harmony in our city and in our world.

I usually teach on the value of racial diversity once or twice a year and insert thoughts on the issue in various messages on love, forgiveness, or unity. We regularly make the weekend in January in which we honor Martin Luther King Jr., who championed racial equality, a day to celebrate our church's racial diversity.

These are not "techniques" for developing racial diversity — they are just actions we take because of what is in our heart. They are things that we do that others may not. A leader said to me once, "You don't get to reach who you *want*, you reach who you *are*." We can lead our congregations and communities into racial harmony if our goal is to bring a little bit of heaven to earth. We can have unity in diversity for the cause of Christ.

Pastor Philip's Final Advice

Ask yourself the hard questions. Give sober answers. Respond and change your world. I really believe that as our churches embrace diversity, the Church can bring healing and wholeness to many of the deep-rooted pains people experience as a result of racial segregation. The Church can and should be leading the way for racial harmony in our world.

My Key Thoughts on Philip's Story

- You will find segregated churches even within an ethnically diverse community.
- It doesn't matter where you are from, but rather where you're going. Central Arkansas to Hollywood.
- Minorities in the Baby Boomer generation and prior still have a tendency to not trust the majority "white" culture and have an even more difficult time with a white leader.
- You should teach and preach the importance of diversity at least twice a year.
- Observation of the MLK holiday is non-negotiable, and a great starting point.
- The church should be the leader in racial harmony and creating cultures that embrace diversity.

The Journey of Forgiveness

Marvin's Story

Pastor Marvin Williams, Trinity Church, Lansing, Michigan

When we stop elevating our vision and our preferences for the Church above HIS VISION for the Church, then I believe we will see more people embracing diversity in the Church.

— Marvin Williams

My journey to the center of church diversity has taken all of my life and counting. I grew up in Chicago and attended a vibrant but traditional black Baptist church. My spiritual and cultural foundation was established at this church. This is where I began my journey with Jesus, was given many leadership opportunities, was trained in evangelism, was taught to be proud of my African American heritage, and ultimately where I accepted my call into ministry. At the request of my pastor and a mentor, I attended and was graduated from Bishop College, a Baptist-affiliated HBCU (Historically Black College/University). God used this experience to help shape and affirm my cultural identity. Upon graduating from

Michigan

Lansing
★

Bishop, my pastor wanted me to attend Howard University for seminary. I refused. I refused, not because Howard was a poor choice; it's a great school. I refused because I sensed in my heart that God wanted to do something different with my ministry, something that was going to require a broader perspective in ministry. So I attendeded and graduated from Trinity Evangelical Divinity School located in Deerfield, Illinois.Trinity helped to equip and affirm my ability to speak and live in black and white. Looking back, I see how God was shaping me for diversity.

Upon completing seminary, the leadership of a large African American church in Grand Rapids called me to be the associate pastor of youth and education. I served for four and one-half years, when the unthinkable happened. The senior pastor died suddenly. We mourned. We cried. Two months later we got up. Because I had faithfully served this congregation, knew the culture and the people, I assumed that the deacons would make a motion to call me as senior pastor and the congregation would affirm their decision. The deacons didn't make the motion and the congregation was divided. I was heartbroken. Ah, but God would move, and He moved in a way I was not expecting. He was about to do something that would change the trajectory of my life and ministry.

Through a number of God-ordained circumstances, I ended up in the office of Ed Dobson, then the senior pastor of Calvary Church (a large predominantly white congregation) of Grand Rapids. We had a growing relationship and I had preached there prior to this meeting. I talked with him about the possibility of planting an African American disciple-making church in Grand Rapids. This seemed to excite him (their church had been praying that God would bring them church planters) and asked me if I would consider coming to Calvary to help with teaching for their popular Saturday night service and then consider planting the church. After praying about it with my wife and receiving counsel from colleagues and friends, I resigned my position at New Hope (in good standing) and accepted the position at Calvary. Some people criticized me for the move, but I knew God was on the move and I had to follow.

During the interview process I found out that prior to me stepping one foot in Ed's office, he'd had a conversation with the executive pastor. He told him when he hired someone for the Saturday night position, to look for someone like Marvin Williams. Not only that, but two months prior to me coming on staff, Ed did an eight-part series on what the Bible says about prejudice and racism. Whoa! Diversity is a God thing. He navigates the circumstances and perfectly positions the right people at the right time for the right moment. I served at Calvary for three years and then God moved us to plant Tabernacle Community Church, a diverse body of believers, whose mission it is to make new and better Christ followers.

When I say God has shaped and is still shaping my heart for diversity in the Church, I am not trying to be super spiritual. Through His providential navigation in my life, developing friendships with people of different cultures, serving in a variety of church settings, and letting His Word and Spirit confront my own prejudices and resistance, God has developed in me a desire to see men and women of different cultures come to know Jesus in deeper ways as they live together, serve together, cry together, laugh together, get angry togther, and love together. This is God's vision for His Church. When we stop elevating our vision and our preferences for the church above HIS VISION for the church, then I believe we will see more people embracing diversity in the Church.

Creating a Culture of Diversity

I know this is going to sound overly spiritual, but when it comes to church diversity, God has to be the one who is doing the creating. Now I am not saying that we should not be intentional in creating a culture of diversity. However, I am saying that the vision of church diversity has to be planted and sealed in the hearts of the cadre of leaders who are leading the church. Over eight years ago I helped (along with two other men and their families) plant a multiethnic church in Grand Rapids, Michigan. A multiethnic church wasn't in the original sketches, however. The original plan was to plant an African American, disciple-making church. Young black families weren't being reached with the gospel and many young people in our community had dropped out of the traditional black church. We wanted to be the bridge, you know, the perennial spiritual gap-fillers in our community. I mean, it made sense to us. We were black, had young families, had fresh ideas about doing church that would connect with those who looked like us, talked like us, joked like us, dressed like us, and shared the same cultural experiences. You know, *our people*. We were simply following the advice of church planting and church growth gurus. We could see and taste the vision of hundreds of young black families and church dropouts coming to know Jesus and growing up in Him. But a fuuny thing happened to us on the way to the office. God messed up our vision for *our church* with a His plan for *His Church*, a diverse church. It was in the praying stages of planting Tabernacle that God began to change our hearts as to what kind of church Tabernacle would be. It was during these times of early morning prayer when God began to slowly melt our hearts and move our lives in the direction of leading a multiethnic church. I believe this prompting was based on God's sovereign purpose mixed with our exposures to and experiences and successes in both cultures in our community. After serving eight years at Tabernacle, God called me to Trinity Church (a large, predominantly white congregation, but growing in diversity) in Lansing, Michigan, to be the senior teaching pastor.

When I was at Tabernacle, the biggest challenges were centered on preferences — music, traditions, preaching style, ministry methods, politics. . . . Our biggest wins were based on the fact that we started this way (diversity was in our DNA) — diverse leadership and ministry teams, diversity on the elder team, diverse small groups, safe and comfortable places for interracial couples. Watching God do deep work in our hearts around diversity, families are serving one another, vacationing together, and doing life together.

At Trinity, we are still on the cusp of understanding what God wants to do with us as it relates to church diversity. A big win for Trinity is having me in the position of senior teaching pastor. This clearly reveals a commitment to embrace diversity at the highest level within the church. Also, we have begun conversations around leadership development, including but not limited to elders, and many of the names on the list are people of color. This simply would not have happened a year ago.

Confront the Elephant in the Pew

This elephant of church diversity has many layers. It seems that when we peel back one layer and have gotten a handle on an issue related to diversity, another layer surfaces. Most Christians just don't have "the cardiovascular endurance" to keep moving the ball of diversity down the field. We like our Christianity easy and "surfacy." What I have found out in this short journey is that we don't want to do the hard work of building deep friendships and understanding the complexity of church diversity.

Second, the elephant is scary and risky. The elephant represents the unknown and we fear the unknown. Will they accept me for who I am? Will they find out about my family history? Do I really know myself? Will assimilation mean losing my identity?

Another reason I believe people are unwilling to confront the elephant of church diversity is because not confronting the elephant is comfortable. We want our Christianity comfortable. The easy chairs in our living rooms have made it difficult for us to follow a Jesus who calls us to discomfort. We don't like to confront the elephant, because it means we will have to confront our own deep prejudices.

Be Intentional

1. Be intentional in creating diverse leadership and ministry teams.
2. Confront the issue head on with creative methods. For a year our small group, which was made up of two white couples, three black couples, and an interracial couple, watched movies and discussed and applied the theological implications. We cried, laughed, affirmed one another, challenged one another, prayed for one another, and vowed that we would never let an elephant like prejudice stand between us.
3. Create diverse small/growth groups.
4. Have friends from various cultures.
5. Make diversity a spiritual dicipline (prayer, Bible reading, simplicity, generosity . . . and diversity).

Pastor Marvin's Final Advice

Let God change your heart through His Word. We have to allow God to step into our lives and critique our lives and the ideologies we hold dear. We have to be willing to allow God's Word to confront pockets of resistance in our lives around this issue. This was made very clear to me after one recent weekend service at Trinity Church (predominantly white, but growing in diversity everyday), the congregation I presently serve as the senior teaching pastor.

During the summer of 2010 we taught through the Old Testament Book of Malachi. The series was called Reset. In the next to the last message, we were resetting justice. The main point of the message was: "Correcting injustice in the world begins with God correcting injustice in me." After the 11:00 service a man approached me and said he needed to ask me to forgive him. Immediately, I wondered what it could be. He told me that when I was introduced as the candidate for the position of senior teaching pastor, he didn't vote for me. "I am sure that many people didn't vote for me," I opined. So his comment was no big revelation to me. What he said next was. He said, "You need to know why I didn't vote for you." I continued to listen. Because of his experiences in the past, he had developed a spirit of prejudice and racism against black people. In essence, he was saying he didn't vote for me because I was black. He began to weep and asked me if I would forgive him. I said it wasn't a problem. He retorted, "Listen! You don't understand. I really need you to forgive me. I don't want the junk of prejudice and racism spilling over into my kids' lives. I didn't vote for you and I was wrong. God has been and is using your preaching to impact my life."

I realized what God was doing. This man heard God and was acting on what he heard. I forgave him. We hugged for a good while, weeping in each other's arms. (Glad we weren't in the men's bathroom doing this — smile! It was a joke!) I was moved and humbled, and I rejoiced as I was reminded that God has me in the right place at the right time doing the right thing. The following week we wrapped up the series and had people share how the series impacted their lives. He stood and shared what God had done and was doing in his heart. The congregation cheered and whistled, and I sensed that God was and is on the move, creating *His Church*.

Start at the top. Hire qualified leaders in key positions. This is not tokenism; this is being intentional.

Be humble. Humility is the foundation of understanding, loving, and embracing people and cultures that are different than ours.

Know that it is not easy. It is complex and it will take time.

Commit to being in it for the long haul. Fighting for and embracing diversity is not for the faint of heart. It takes tenacity, humility, honesty, transparency, and a commitment to building deep friendships.

My Key Thoughts on Marvin's Story

- Our life experiences with people, places, and things shape our hearts for diversity.
- Don't simply listen to the church planting, church growth, and business experts — listen to God!
- A few small pushes on your individual church diversity story will begin to affect an entire congregation and help shape the *big* picture.
- Make diversity a spiritual discipline — a discipline to help us become more like Jesus.
- Church diversity has layers. Commit to peeling them back one at a time.

We Are Church Diversity!

Just as these individual stories matter to the *big* picture, each and every one of our stories matter as well. These stories are all vastly different and the one common theme that each story had was this: leaders with hearts to embrace diversity and place God's agenda ahead of their own agenda. The diversity fire started burning deep in the hearts of these leaders. Intentionality and "Do the

Right Thing Leadership" continued to fan the flame. You have a diversity story to tell. What will your story be? Will it be riddled with woulda, coulda, shoulda, but never dida, or will it begin with "A defining moment for me as it relates to embracing diversity in the church was. . . ." Tell your story, live your story, share your story. You are church diversity. I am church diversity. *We are church diversity!*

CHURCH DIVERSITY CHALLENGE 6

Which of these stories most impacted the way you currently view church diversity? How did they impact you?

What is your story when it comes to diversity in your church? If you do not have a story, what are some things you can do to start your story?

Why is it so critical that leaders be intentional when embracing diversity within their church?

Pray and ask God what He wants diversity to look like in your church. What is He telling you?

What are some specific changes in thinking you need to make in order to create a more diverse environment in your church based upon what you learned from these pastors' stories?

Endnotes
1. Bill Hybels, *Courageous Leadership* (Grand Rapids, MI: Zondervan, 2009).
2. Ibid.

7 Diversity in Worship

*Worship is the one thing that is designed
to bring us all together.*

— Israel Houghton

*Winning dove awards, #1 songs on the radio, and
thousands of records sold all paled in
comparison to the feeling I had when I stood on
stage with a diverse group of worshipers.*

— Chuck Dennie

Check out video 7
www.nlpg.com/churchdiversity

I originally intended for this chapter to be a section of chapter 6; however, I thought it would be better served as a stand-alone. As I was reading the stories from so many great pastors, I noticed that a common thread to a successfully diverse church is diversity in worship.

Pastor Femi from Nigeria stated, "Music and rhythm are very crucial in our culture — so we are very intentional and deliberately weave in songs from various tribal languages in our worship experiences. It's amazing to see how people easily connect seeing other people not from their tribe, worshiping God in their dialect. It creates an atmosphere of unity."

Femi's statement reminds me of when my wife LaKendria and I originally transitioned from Gospel music to the perceived "rock concert" we were confronted with when we began attending LifeChurch.tv. My wife grew up singing in church, and I remember my father-in-law encouraging us to find a church home where she could share "her gift." Yes, my wife can sing. Once we got plugged into LifeChurch.tv, I had to chuckle at the potential of her singing. My wife singing and LifeChurch.tv didn't seem to make sense, and my wife was totally content with that being a childhood gift that she left in her childhood. Although I'm an extrovert and prefer to be an up-front-on-the-stage kind of guy, my bride is an introvert and is perfectly content with being behind the scenes.

I wish I could honestly say that we were open recipients to this new contemporary worship style of music. Sorry, it just felt rhythmless and emotionless. We would actually get to church about 15 minutes late because we knew that we would probably miss the majority of the concert — I mean worship service. When we invited people to church, we would often tell them that they would have to excuse the music. We weren't trying to be disparaging of LifeChurch.tv worship, it was a matter of perspective and preference. We were just well aware of the harsh reality that the difference in worship style was going to be a problem for many of our Gospel music–loving friends and family that we invited to church.

Over the years, God began to soften our hearts and if I'm going to be forthright, one of the first times the worship really caught my attention was when I saw an African American drummer. This holds true to the theories presented in previous chapters about the importance of people seeing themselves represented on the platform or in some perceived formal leadership capacity. The drummer's presence communicated that maybe this music isn't so bad and maybe a black guy can appreciate this worship genre. Over the years we have grown to embrace the fact that contemporary Christian music not only has rhythm and emotion but rather all worship music is a continuation of communion with God. Worship is not about what I go in the doors and receive, but rather what I can go in the doors and give. I get the opportunity to give God my worship. Tomlin, Sapp, Hillsong, and Lacrae are mere tools to help me worship the God of the universe.

I now have a clearer understanding of what it means to worship out of the overflow and embrace what Pastor Femi stated. I can "easily connect seeing other people not from my tribe [or worship music style] worshiping God in their dialect. It creates an atmosphere of unity." God has really broadened my iTunes playlist — Gospel, contemporary Christian, Christian rap, hip-hop, R & B, classical, blues — you name it and I probably listen to it. The only music that I really don't connect with is country music. I think my nasty roomate with the 20-ounce soda pop bottle spittoon turned me off to all things country. Not really; well, kinda. I do periodically listen to country music, because a friend from my LifeGroup is the morning radio host "Joe Friday" on the local Oklahoma City country station, the Twister.

When I was hired at LifeChurch.tv, God really thrust me into a major crash course worship leadership class. I had to lead worship leaders who led in a music genre that I wasn't totally a fan of and for the most part didn't understand. Again, through leading, listening, praying, and growing, God gave me an understanding of the value of worship as a universal language of love. I have provided direct leadership to several worship leaders over the last five years and have been able to demonstrate the importance of embracing a culture of diversity. Each of my different worship leaders instilled the principle of creating a culture of diversity in their own unique way. None of them had ever been asked, encouraged, or forced to wrestle with the concept prior to being a part of my team. It doesn't matter where you're from, it matters where you're going. Each of these guys changed their perspective and changed the game for the people attending each and every week. Probably even changed generational thinking. We grew in the overall area of understanding diversity in the context of worship each and every year. As the worship leaders from my team would move to different areas of the organization or to different churches, God would send someone else with an open heart ready and willing to beat for diversity.

When my man Andy Kirk came on board, our worship team began to show some early signs of gaining diversity traction. Andy was a young 20-year-old up-and-coming worship leader/Christian recording artist who was open to listening and learning. God spoke, and we all listened. Andy was eventually called back to his home area of Nashville, Tennessee, to plug into a local church and finish his latest record deal. After Andy's departure, I hired a veteran worship leader and national Christian recording artist, Chuck Dennie. Chuck had previously been on staff at another location at LifeChurch.tv about four years prior to joining our team. Chuck was the lead singer of the band By the Tree and was known for his hit song "Beautiful One." That's the song that just won't go away. As a matter of fact, it popped up on my Pandora playlist about an hour ago. Chuck was a great leader to work with. He had senior pastor–type leadership qualities, and his worship leadership style included teaching, leading, and for the most part, demanding a culture of worship. Chuck led and people worshiped. Not only did people worship, but they were able to worship with a diverse group of worshipers on stage. No matter who was coming through our doors, they would have some representation of themselves on the stage. The number of people that we had on our worship team doubled under Chuck's leadership. This exponentially increased the potential for "all people" to be represented on stage. We were on a worship roll, hitting on all cylinders, and then guess what happened? God showed up.

As in the previous chapter, I'm going to have a few worship leaders share their thoughts on diversity, specifically as it relates to worship.

God Showed Up (Chuck Dennie)

There is a common phrase that we use in church when we experience God in a service. We say, "God showed up." The truth is, He was always there — we just finally experienced Him. For ten years I had the privilege of traveling the world as a worship leader and recording artist with the band By the Tree. It wasn't until I served under Pastor Scott

Williams' leadership that my eyes were opened to diversity. Sure, diversity was and is all around me, but it wasn't until Scott helped me see it that it became an integral part of my ministry.

I grew up in a small town where the only color besides white in my community was on the small building by the train track. This building was a staple in the community, as people would paint different Happy Birthday wishes on the side of it. Unfortunately, I wasn't afforded the privilege of growing up with a diverse group of people of different races. Because of the fact that my eyes had not yet opened to the beauty found in diversity, my God-given talent and art was one color.

The sad fact is that for nearly the first 32 years of my life, no one ever told me or expressed how important diversity was — especially in the Church! That all changed when I met Scott. It's often said that leadership is caught, not taught, and that is representative of my time serving as Scott's worship leader. He never told me to gather a diverse team of musicians and singers on the stage, but after a few short months that is just what God had done at our campus. Scott's heart for diversity was contagious, and God used his leadership and passion for diversity to open my eyes and see the beauty diversity brings. We assembled a worship team with Hispanic, white, Asian, and black individuals all represented, and when we joined together on the stage I truly felt that the heart of God was represented. Winning Dove awards, #1 songs on the radio, and thousands of records sold all paled in comparison to the feeling I had when I stood on stage with a diverse group of worshipers that happened to be musicians and singers. The beauty of us leading and worshiping Jesus together has to be a glimpse of what heaven will be like.

I am now a campus pastor with LifeChurch.tv, outside of Nashville, Tennessee. Each and every Sunday I thank God for Scott's leadership in my life, because I am now aware of the importance of diversity. I continually pray that God will send us different ethnicities and refuse to use excuses of why it will not happen. Diversity is all around us, but it is impossible to see if we are not aware of the importance. As the leader of a campus, I hope to show others how beautiful diversity truly is. I thank Scott for his leadership and heart to see things how they can be, and not as they are. Scott's desire to see the Church move from where it is to where it needs to be has inspired me to do the same. There is one more leader residing in a suburb of Nashville, committed to running alongside leaders like Scott and everyone who has a heart for embracing diversity. We will see it become a reality in the Church.

People's Church

I featured Herbert's story from the People's Church in chapter 6. Herbert is a great friend, gifted communicator, awesome leader, and the real-deal when it comes to church diversity. Herbert is quietly and boldly leading a diverse church in what would be stereotyped as an unlikely city. I have had the opportunity to watch People's Church explode right here in my city. If you ask anyone in Oklahoma City where the multiethnic or diverse church is, they will first point you to People's Church.

I have had the opportunity over the years to develop great relationships with Herbert's leadership team. One of the guys that I have had the opportunity to watch from afar is Brian Rush. Brian has grown from the worship leader to the director of creative arts. I have always been impressed with Brian's leadership, humility, and creativity. This guy has led some of the most culturally diverse and creative experiences that I have seen in the last couple of years. You heard from Herbert and now I would like you to hear the fact that "it's not about you" from Brian.

It's Not about You — It's about Them (Brian Rush)

Before coming to People's Church, I had not really thought that much about music and worship from a multicultural sense. Throughout my life I've always had friends of different cultures, but I had never been in a church setting where there was a great mix of multiple cultures. Most of the issues I faced musically in the church involved traditional music versus contemporary. That was completely thrown out the door at People's Church. It was now a matter of how does this white boy from small-town Oklahoma connect with a broad audience (age, culture, background, style, etc.) of believers and unbelievers who want to connect with God through music? How do I find musicians who can play all this diverse music? Will I be laughed off the stage when I try to pull this off? How do you smoothly transition a rock tune, which is usually written in sharps, to a Gospel tune that is most often written in flats? The answer to all of these questions is *you just do*!

We can make excuses all day, every day, about why something won't work, but in the end you just have to make up your mind to find a way and then make it happen. Sometimes it can be so easy to get used to doing something a certain way that you just don't think about doing it differently. I see this with musicians all the time who come to our place thinking they are pretty good players, and they are, but usually at only a couple of styles of music. After they are on our team for a couple weeks they will come up to me and say something like, "Dude, I'm really being stretched as a musician. I've never played stuff like this before." I love it because it opens their hearts up to new things and stretches them as a musician and follower of Christ. When we first started out, it was myself leading worship (and running sound) from the keyboards, a drummer, and a couple of back-up singers. Fast forward eight years into the life of our church — the musicians and vocalists came, I figured out how to sing with some soul (thanks in part to all the Stevie Wonder and Michael Jackson I listened to growing up), and God assembled a dream team of diverse people with like-minded hearts to advance the Kingdom.

When you look at our worship team, you see a lot of very different people. Different skin color, different ages, different musical tastes, different backgrounds, different hair, etc. What you also see is a group of people that is completely committed to seeing the vision of a multicultural church come to pass and change the world for Jesus. Something I tell our team all the time, and that I've believed from the very beginning, is that "I'll take heart over talent every time." Someone may be great at what they do, but if they don't own the heart and vision of People's Church, then they probably won't last very long. Opinions can be pretty intense especially when it comes to music, and I want people on our team that feel the mission/vision is more important than what they simply prefer for themselves.

Something that our Senior Pastor Herbert Cooper says often is that "you have to give up what you love for what you love more." Do I have a favorite style of music that I prefer? Sure. Is that the most important thing? *No way!* Would it be easier to play just one style of music? Probably. Is that the best thing for our church? Nope. When I'm planning a set-list of music, can I just keep people in mind that are like me? I guess. Does that honor God and advance His Kingdom? Probably not.

What is fascinating is that once you are intentionally in an environment of diversity you find there are many things that you thought you did or didn't like that end up being things that you really do love. I love the huge anthems of Hillsong United *and* I love the powerful simplicity of songs like Marvin Sapp's "Never Would Have Made It," and you know what? We sing both of them! Sometimes in the same set right next to each other. It's incredible to see God moving in people's hearts as we sing all these songs each week. Red, yellow, black, and white, all in chorus together. Old songs, new songs, Latin beats, gospel grooves, rock 'n' roll riffs, and everything in between. It really is a matter of the heart.

We have been very intentional not only with our worship teams, but with our entire church, to teach and speak often about the fact that "it is not about you, it's about them." It's about those who have not heard the gospel; it's about casting a net wide enough to bring in *all* types of fish whatever that may look like. If it ever becomes just about us, then it's time to close the doors. I've never read a Scripture that says the angels in heaven rejoice when you play an incredible lead guitar solo or break down the house with an amazing Gospel vocal run (even though both are great). I do remember reading something about the angels in heaven rejoicing over that one lost soul that finds God. You've got to give up what you love for what you love more.

Music Has No Color (Marc Milan)

You've likely heard it said that music is a universal language. Through my experiences in leading worship, I have seen how music can soften the hardest heart and comfort a wounded soul. I truly believe that "music has no color" and doesn't discriminate. My heart and passion is to help a diverse group of people connect with God through music and create environments of worship. I was born and raised in the Bronx — a Puerto Rican kid growing up in a big city. The Bronx is a place rich in all types of diversity: food, style, language, and culture. When I moved to South Florida, I discovered that diversity was just about as likely as a pipe organ in a Baptist church in Georgia. Everyone on the platform and in the seats looked the same for the most part. This reality forces you to wrestle with the question of "Am I in the right place?"

When I was on staff at Potential Church, Pastor Troy Gramling would always say, "Diversity takes intentionality." He was absolutely right. We intentionally scheduled singers and musicians that were not all the same race so that our platform reflected diversity. The reason? People who visit any given church tend to identify with those who are on the platform, and if those who are on the platform all look the same or just represent a certain culture, we (the leaders) have missed a great opportunity to tear down some walls. When I moved to West Palm Beach, Florida, I again saw the opportunity for diversity as the worship leader at South Palm Community Church (South Palm).

Unlike Potential Church, which has diversity as a part of their DNA and core values, South Palm did not have a culture of diversity. We began to show diversity in transitional videos, Scripture reading that spoke to the heart of diversity, and being intentional with the overall service. Eventually we began to see the difference it made in the people who began to attend and remain in our church. The truth of the matter is this: if you take a look at your congregation and see only one demographic represented, you should take stock of what you're doing. Take a good look at your platform. Your platform representation is inadvertently communicating who is welcome in your church. Your platform is communicating "This is who is welcome here."

I currently lead worship at the Crossing Church in Tampa, Florida. We have a lot of diversity, with both English and Spanish campuses. Our worship vision is to represent diversity in sound as well. We incorporate musical styles with Latin flava, pop/gospel, and rock spread throughout the month. Our directional leadership team for the entire church is diverse. Lead Pastor Greg Dumas embraces a culture of diversity and believes that all people are welcome and all are gifted to serve. We want to add diversity in as many places as possible within our church. We desire to impact our city through the diverse people in our community.

The only way this works is through leadership, as people come to our churches and they see diversity in our platforms and in the positions of leadership, then people begin to realize and understand that they are valued and loved in that place. I have personally seen how the simple act of intentional diversity can impact the person or the family that walks through the door once the first worship song starts. There is great love displayed in diversity. It shows unity, it shows that we are all God's children. It really reveals the message of true love. On a creative level, I have also seen the value of diversity in team settings. There is so much value added to the dimensions of ideas when we have diverse group of people at the table. We not only have different ideas coming to the forefront, we have something greater: a fresh perspective and new eyes to help us see how things translate to different people, and by having this valuable information, hopefully, together, we all can reach more people for the Kingdom of God.

I do believe music is the universal language and that it has no color, so it's important that we don't place a color on it. We instead must be intentional about reaching different people within the community by allowing diversity to become a reality on our teams, our platform, and the people we serve with.

Thoughts from Grammy Award–Winner Israel Houghton
Love God, Love People

In my personal opinion, one of the best-known worship leaders living out and understanding the importance of embracing diversity is Israel Houghton. Israel Houghton is known for injecting contemporary gospel and worship with a blazing, youthful energy that has made him among the most influential worship leaders on the planet. As a singer, composer, multi-instrumentalist, producer, and worship leader, he has created a canon of songs that have become standards in churches around the globe. He accomplished much worship influence as the leader of Israel and New Breed, a Grammy, Stellar, and Dove Award–winning musical ensemble and ministry organization that has amassed gold-selling albums and critical platitudes reserved for the best of the best.

Over the years, Israel has amassed a legion of fans while blasting down musical barriers and drawing together people of all races, ages, and cultures through worship. Israel's solo projects have even helped the world of worshipers understand that worship is a universal language and, in my opinion, a language of love. His most recent project, "Love God, Love People," is a return to a simple, foundational gospel command: "Love the Lord your God with all your heart and your neighbor as yourself," says Israel. "Virtually every song touches on this profound simplicity. It all comes down to 'love God, love people.' Period." He has said this about his music in the past, "It's not a white sound or black sound, it's a Kingdom sound." These two points are crucial for worship leaders, and all ministry leaders, for that matter. Our worship music and our preaching are based on the basic Christian tenet of loving God and loving people. Second, our music and teaching is about Kingdom impact, "Big K," and not just impacting our little sphere. Those principles allow us to think *bigger*. Ministry leaders and worship leaders will think *big* when it comes to the number of people who are attending their church or the number of people raising their hands in the air during worship. A more important thought and concern for worship leaders to wrestle with is this: "Is my music, my heart, my style, and my message about reaching all people for Jesus — or simply some people?" Think *big* and wrestle with that one!

Israel has wrestled with that question for the more than 20 years that he has been in full-time ministry. Throughout those years, the boxes that people tend to put up always intrigued him. Many of the boxes he is referring to are based on skin tone, culture, and even theology. Unfortunately, within "the Church" there are so many things that separate us and create divisive wedges. Israel truly believes that "worship is the one thing that is designed to bring us all together." I totally agree, because worship is a universal language.

Israel found it amazing that everyone was always comfortable with this sectioned-off mentality. Israel is half black and half white and was raised in a white family in a Hispanic culture and church. He admits that his background and culture allow him to come by diversity very honestly. He has had many different influences musically and stylistically.

An important statement that Israel makes as it relates to his calling as a worship leader is this, "If my calling is to be a worship leader, I want to have some real intention and purpose behind it. I want at least one of the flags that I'm waving to be about tearing down some of those boxes and bringing people who would not have normally come together, together."

Israel encourages leaders who are trying to introduce diversity into their context to understand that doing so has to be a cause and something that consumes you. He understands that everyone may not feel that sense of calling. As for him and his house, he wants to make sure that they are doing it. If leaders are interested in exploring and reaching beyond their particular demographic, they must understand that a lot of it has to do with music and it also has to do with leadership. This is something that has to be flowing out of the leader. The leader has to staff the worship team with people that all people can see themselves in. This intentionality and staffing will always prove to be a major catalyst for change. Israel talks about worship preference from a heavenly perspective by saying, "When we get to heaven, no one is going to be there with a clipboard saying, 'Now which section would you feel most comfortable in?' "

Israel's heart for diversity bleeds over into his diverse fan base. He has been featured on FOX, CBS, ABC, BET, CNN, TBN, and CBN, and has amassed a legion of followers that crosses generational lines with popularity among African

American, Latin, and Caucasian fans. His music and heart continue to break down would-be ethnic and style barriers. Receiving two gold-selling albums, three Grammy Awards, six Dove Awards, two Stellar Awards, and a Soul Train Award has fittingly awarded his diversity success.

A Universal Language

One morning at my church one of the young couples that attend came up and introduced me to the wife's mother who was visiting from Kenya. Her daughter had recently had a baby and she was going to be in the United States visiting for a couple of months. As I visited with the mom in her traditional Kenya attire and welcomed her at the entryway of the church, I watched as she scanned our lobby, church, and the people. I remember sitting in the back as our worship team sang these lyrics to the Hillsong United Song "The Stand": "I'll stand with arms high and heart abandoned . . . in awe of the One who gave it all." The genre, style, or part of the world did not matter at that moment. All that mattered was worshiping the King of kings, whose worship is a universal love language. This elderly Kenyan lady raised her hands high and you could clearly see that she was lost in worship and vividly moved by the One who gave it all. My heart was in awe and a huge smile was plastered across my face as I imagined what heaven would be like.

What About Worship?

In my opinion, worship is a key component to the overall church diversity conversation and movement. Diversity in worship matters, and there is definitely more than one theory on creating diversity in music, worship experiences, and praise and worship. I have heard many different theories and processes for being intentional in the worship (meaning musical) part of a service. I know of one church whose criteria for the worship leader's selection of music is this: young, old, black, and white. That's their philosophy and the filter for every single worship set they do every single weekend. They ask the question of whether the songs appeal to young, old, black, and white people. Another church has a more extensive practice. They have four worship team leaders — two white and two black. Each week they will rate a song with a score of 1 to 10, with 1 being the most contemporary rockin' song imaginable, and 10 being the most Gospel of Gospel songs. If the average score is not between a 4 and 6, they don't play it . . . period. Other churches simply map out a month's worth of set lists and make sure that they are weaving diversity in and out of the four weeks. Some churches will not change their contemporary style but incorporate hip-hop, spoken word, variety, visual elements, and so on to represent diversity. No matter the diversity within the musical selection, media elements and worship team members go a long way. You can never discount the value of having diverse representation on your stage. Remember, it was the black drummer who helped soften my heart to the worship music, style, and genre that I have now grown to love.

There is no right or wrong way to incorporate diversity into worship. None of the above methods are extreme or inadequate — they are simply methods of intentionality. Remember, it's not how you get from where you are to where you need to be, but the fact that you are on the journey. Some people believe in the "extreme or not at all" method, and I personally believe that doesn't get us anywhere. The approach that we use at LifeChurch.tv NW, "the N-Dub," is more along the lines of incorporating hip-hop, spoken word, variety, visual elements, and a very diverse worship team to represent diversity.

Worship leaders love wearing the badges of "creative" and "innovative." Rightfully so, as worship leaders and music directors are some of the most innovative and creative people in the church. *Innovative* is defined simply as the act of introducing something new. *Creative* is defined as having the ability to create, characterized by originality of thought. I am an adamant believer that if a worship leader wants to be a driving force in the area of innovation, he or she must have a diverse team of worshipers. If you have a bunch of guys and gals standing around the platform that all look alike, think alike, and have similar life experiences, it's only a matter of time before new ideas are just recycled ideas. By recycled I mean "more of the same."

The local church is the hope of the world and the future rests partially in the innovative and creative hands of its worship leaders. If you want to wear the badge of "creative," it's time get imaginative. Seek God, ask Him to give you a heart for diversity, pray for a diverse worship team, and pray for your unique opportunity to bring diversity to your church. There are thousands of worship leaders with hearts that embrace diversity that are poised to impact the future of worship in the Church. I can promise you that worship leaders can be more creative than having a musical set list that includes two fast songs, one slow song, and then closing with one fast song or whatever that "business as usual" set list would be for your context. There is nothing better than genuine, authentic worship. Authentic worship with some semblance of diversity makes it that much better.

Every success story begins with the desire to try and the desire to take a step. Take the step!

CHURCH DIVERSITY CHALLENGE 7

What does worship mean to you and how have you used it in your church to connect your congregation with God?

How does your worship represent a spirit of diversity in your church? In what ways can you improve?

What style of worship music do you prefer? What specifically connects you to that particular style of music?

How could embracing more diversity in your worship help your church boldly confront the elephant in the pew?

Does your worship strive to reach just certain groups of people at your church or all people? What specific changes do you need to make immediately to begin the process of reaching all people through your worship?

What challenges will you face as your begin to embrace diversity in your worship? Are you prepared to meet those challenges?

Back to the Basics — the ABCs of Church Diversity

Willingness to share the teaching responsibilities with a minority is the ultimate church diversity litmus test for any church or ministry leader.

— Scott Williams

Check out video 8
www.nlpg.com/churchdiversity

I want to thank you for taking this journey down what is known as an awkward road for most people. Once you travel down an awkward road and face the brutal facts along the way, it becomes less and less awkward. I pray that God is using these stories, perspectives, words, and pages to soften your heart toward this issue of church diversity. By making it to this final chapter you are already primed to be a pivotal change agent for God's chosen vessel, the local church.

My friends, church diversity is not an easy issue to discuss or confront. Part of the difficulty is the fact that there are three things in life that we are "not supposed" to talk about. What are those three things you might ask. We are not supposed to talk about race, religion, and politics. Unfortunately for the Church and the subject of church diversity, two of the three "no-no" topics are front and center.

This final chapter will bring everything full-circle and provide practical steps to make the necessary changes and begin the necessary conversations. The ABCs of church diversity are derived from the acronym Assess → Believe → Change!

This chapter will provide some stimulating questions to help ministries, congregants, and communities honestly *Assess* where they are regarding church diversity. I will outline what it means to truly embrace diversity instead of simply tolerating it. This embracing mindset will reinforce the importance of diversity in the Church and help God's children understand and *Believe* that having a heart for church diversity is biblical, necessary, and the right thing to do. I pray that you will walk away *Believing* that your role matters. You are in the minority of Christians by being a part of this movement. You are on the ground floor of a movement and work of God that will change the heart, face, and future of the Church. Last, you will be challenged to begin implementing the *Change*. You are the change that God is looking for.

We will look at some thought-provoking ideas and practical solutions to make this change a lasting reality. The amazing aspect of this entire discussion is that we get to be on the front lines of this movement. We get to take a peek into the future and imagine how different the Church will look once this *Change* begins to happen. Imagine this beautiful possibility for a moment: 40 years from now we could look at the Church and Dr. King's words — "We must face the sad fact that at the eleven o' clock hour on Sunday morning when we stand to sing, we stand in the most segregated hour in America" — would be hard to believe and even laughable. You will be a part of Christians around the globe saying, "Remember when the church was segregated? That's hard to believe. How could our parents and grandparents have been so blind?"

I have conversations with my mom all the time about her experiences in the 1950s and 1960s. That was just about 50 years ago and it's difficult for me to fathom the things she had to experience. She got her food at the back door of restaurants, attended segregated schools, sat in the balcony at a movie theater, and was banned from public restrooms, all because of the color of her skin. Every time I think about that I'm truly baffled at how ridiculous it sounds. If I'm being honest, the fact that church is still the most segregated institution in America and possibly the world is equally as ridiculous and baffling.

We live in a nation that has an African American president, integration is all around us, and overall diversity is a growing value. The Church has run out of excuses and frankly, we are running out of time. If you don't take anything away from this book, I want you to walk away knowing that *Change* begins with us and *Change* begins now. We are the change that God is looking for. God's word is clear, He is simply looking for His people to stand up and say "no more!" You are a change agent; God has chosen you to be a part of this movement — the first of its kind in the last 40 years. I just wish for a moment you could feel this God-birthed passion inside of me about this subject. Thinking of our nation's history, my family's history, my mom's experiences, and the potential for the future of the Church is overwhelming. I'm in tears as I type this sentence. It's just stupid, my friends. As Christians, we have the answers. God's Word has given us a clear direction, yet we make excuses.

I'm sitting in my office now looking at all of the amazing books on my bookshelf, many of which have provided ideas, strategies, techniques, theories, and suggestions for me personally, my business, and the Church to be better. I'm seriously staring at rows of books from some of my favorite authors and although they all serve a great purpose, their purpose is definitely not more important than integrating God's Church. If we are truly about reaching all people for Jesus, there can't be a more important topic for us to talk about than church diversity. Leaders move people from where they are to where they need to be. God is leading. Are you ready? Let's go!

Assess

The assessment part of the process is the most critical. This is where congregants, ministry leaders, denominational leaders, and Christians-at-large assess *themselves*. This self-assessment process is about asking the gut-level honest questions as to where you and your church stand regarding church diversity. This is when you look in the mirror and ask God to reveal your heart on this issue. I am going to provide some questions for you and your church to ponder. I will answer the questions myself as honestly as possible and challenge you to do the same. My answers are never to be critical but rather to assess where we are and look forward to where we can be. When you assess your church, be honest and unashamed. There is only a small but growing percentage of churches that are having success. It takes time. I will first provide a self-assessment and then an assessment for the Church. Remember, there are no right or wrong answers; the most important thing is to simply be honest.

Self-Assessment

1. What is my history in dealing with issues of race and ethnicity? For me personally, the answer to this question is quite simple. I have always been in the minority culture at school and work. The barbershop doesn't count, because black people have a special kind of hair that needs to be cut by a special kind of barber. I will have to draw a line in the sand and remain segregated on my barbershop experience. In all seriousness, the only place that I've been a part of the majority culture outside of family is Sunday mornings, at various predominantly African American churches I've attended over the years. I have always been sensitive to issues of race and ethnicity.

2. How has racial prejudice reared its face in my life? Again, I have always been the minority. Being in the minority position and growing up when people dropped the "N-word" to me or around me always created these unspoken thoughts of prejudice. The bottom line is, I'm different, you are different; I do things this way and you do things that way. "White people" do XYZ and black people don't. That's the filter that shaped part of my thinking. It also didn't help that I am simply one generation removed from a mother who faced blatant racial prejudice and injustice. The reality is that those experiences and thoughts from my family and friends shaped my opinions of the majority culture, which happened to be white. It was really easy to grab on to "the white man is holding me down syndrome" that plagues all too many minorities. I was blessed with a great family and a mother who encouraged me to dream *big* and think *bigger*. She challenged us to embrace the realities for what they are and press forward to what can be and what will be. Our home, friends, and life communicated that we loved all people and all people had the potential for good. We embraced diversity.

Don't get me wrong, that didn't negate the conversations fueled by the harsh realities I've faced because I'm a minority. To act as though prejudice and racism aren't real and everything is hunky-dory isn't the answer. Makeshift reality doesn't help anyone and definitely doesn't help get us to where we need to be. I am regularly faced with decisions that run through the diversity grid. In the midst of writing this book we were dealing with transferring my oldest son Wesley to Cheyenne Middle School, which is located just outside of our local district. Middle school was a new venture, so we wanted to give him a jumpstart with a great school to kick off his new middle school career. We had heard a few negative things about Summit Middle School, which was the school that he was supposed to attend. After completing the transfer and after Wesley attended Cheyenne for about a week, we were faced with the decision of whether to stay or go. The child of the family we were car-pooling with was not connecting with kids at Cheyenne, so they decided to move him back to Summit. After going back and forth and spending time at both schools, the supposed issues boiled down to perception reality and diversity. Wesley brought it to my attention one morning as we were talking through our decision as a family. He said, "Dad, we are talking about diversity. What's wrong with diversity? Aren't you writing a book on diversity?" Ouch, gut check, heart check, and reality check. We moved Wesley to Summit and he has loved it, we have loved it, and the diversity will continue to shape him and us alike. The beauty of the position that I find myself in right now is the fact that my experiences, realities, and calling can help provide one roadmap for how we can propel the Bride of Christ to where she needs to be.

3. Do I have genuine relationships with people of different races and ethnicities? I can honestly answer this question with a yes for as long as I can remember. I have had seasons throughout my years of leaning toward and hanging with one ethnic group or the other; however, my relationships always remained diverse. My small group is racially diverse, my staff team is diverse, my friends are diverse, and my particular campus (church) is growing in diversity.

A great way to help with the self-assessment of the genuine diversity in your relationships is what is known as the *Cell Phone Test*. What is the Cell Phone Test? Right now as you are reading this I want you to stop and take out your cell phone before you read the next sentence. (Pick up your cell phone.) Seriously, we are going to pause right here until you have your cell phone. Once you have it in your hand, proceed with your reading. Now turn to your contacts. Slowly scroll through your contacts and see how many diverse names are in your phone. To take it a step further, ask this question, "How many of the people on my contact list that don't look like me have I called and talked to in the last month?" If you are thinking right now about the diverse relationships that you have and thinking that they all revolve around people that you work with, the question to ponder further is, "Are my diverse work relationships turning into doing life together outside of work?" It's the heart of the message that Pastor John Bryson communicated in the portion of chapter 6 titled "Lives and Dinner Tables Diversified."

Church Assessment

The church assessment is difficult for congregants, ministry leaders, denominational heads, and senior pastors alike. It's easy to point out what the churches around the corner are doing or not doing, but looking at our own church sometimes hurts. When you conduct the church assessment, remember it's not about right or wrong, good or bad, but rather an honest assessment. Again, this is not the time for ministry leaders to start beating themselves up. It's an opportunity to honestly assess where their church is and begin asking God to reveal a plan to get where they need to be.

Congregants play an important role in the church assessment process. The primary evangelistic tool for any church is personal invitations from existing congregants. Billboards, mailers, advertisements, commercials, and outreach are all tools for getting people through the doors of a church; however, those are generally a complement to a personal invitation. More often than not, they have seen the mailer, they have heard the commercials, they have heard the stories, and then someone extended a personal invite and they decided to visit "XYZ Church" for the very first time.

If congregants don't feel that their friends will feel totally welcomed at their church, they won't invite them. Instead they will recommend the church around the corner. I have been guilty of this for as long as I can remember. I would attend a predominantly black church, and I would invite my white friends to the predominantly white church across town where I thought they would feel welcome and connect. Even when I first began attending LifeChurch.tv, although I loved the ministry, I would invite my black friends to the predominantly black churches around Oklahoma City.

Early on, I was not totally comfortable that people I invited would feel welcome. Over the years I would communicate all of the amazing things that we loved about the church: biblical teaching, life applicable message, casual dress, the amazing children's ministry, and the ability to get plugged in and serve. I would always share the caveat that there are not very many minorities and the music is rock 'n' roll. As a congregant, I was always doing a personal church assessment before I felt comfortable inviting them to my church. Fast forward eight years, and we have been intentional about creating a culture that embraces diversity at the NW Oklahoma City Campus of LifeChurch.tv. I feel totally comfortable inviting anyone of any race, socio-economic status, and background to our campus (i.e., all people). I would also be confident that they would feel welcome. Not only would they feel welcome, they would almost be guaranteed to see minorities and people that look like them. Unfortunately that's not the case for most churches. That is not a critical statement, but rather an illustration of the great importance for congregants and leaders to begin these conversations and conduct these assessments.

As far as ministry leaders are concerned, it's even more important for us to conduct a self-assessment for our church. Not only are we the ones steering the ship, we are held to a higher standard. Read through these church assessment questions and answer them honestly. The harsh realities may be convicting, and that's just part of the process.

Church Assessment

1. Is ethnic diversity represented at the highest level of leadership within my church? Denominational leaders might ask an additional question: is ethnic diversity represented at the highest leadership team within our denomination?

I will answer this question in two parts as it relates to my church. LifeChurch.tv is a multisite church with 14 (and counting) campuses around the country. As a matter of fact, I can almost guarantee that by the time you have this book in your hand, LifeChurch.tv will have another campus up and rolling. Our board of directors, which is an advisory board consisting of senior pastors from around the country, lay leaders, and the LifeChurch.tv directional leadership team, has one minority: Herbert Cooper, senior pastor of People's Church, featured in chapter 6. Our Directional Leadership Team (DLT) consists of five leaders, one being our senior pastor, Craig Groeschel. Each of these five leaders has a specific area of responsibility and an equal voice. Although they have an equal voice, as Pastor Craig puts it, "I still reserve the right to make the hard call." The DLT sets the leadership and direction of our church. Although this board has age and experience diversity, this team does not have any ethnic diversity represented on it. Of the 14 campus pastors, there are two minorities: one of our campus pastors in Tulsa, Tome Dawson (Asian), and myself (black).

My staff does have ethnic diversity represented; the representation, including myself, is about one-third of my staff team. That number is consistent, even with transition of team members to other campuses and other churches. We have had East Indian, Latino, and African American team members. As we look at teams at the highest level, when possible it's important to have diversity. Not only does it help foster the right conversation at the highest levels, it communicates volumes to the church and generally helps with the hiring and promotion of minorities.

2. Are the recruitment and hiring practices for staff, as well as volunteer placement strategies, sensitive to diversity?

I truly believe our HR leadership team director has a heart for having a diverse staff culture; however, we are just beginning to gain a small amount of momentum in this area. For the longest time, there have only been a handful of minorities represented on the LifeChurch.tv team as a whole. Pastor Craig handpicked several of the tenured minority staff, including myself. Out of roughly 260 full- and part-time staff members, roughly 22 are ethnic minority. Nearly half of those staff are actually members of the two campuses that I have mentioned in this book — the Campus that I lead (NW Oklahoma City Campus) and the campus Trevor leads (South Oklahoma City Campus).

The positive, as it relates to minority staffing at LifeChurch.tv, is the fact that about 25 percent of those team members have come on staff in the last year. That definitely demonstrates progress and intentionality. It's important for that progress to expand to the broader team. It's always great to have diversity represented in your media design and graphic arts teams, as it creates variety from a visual and experiential perspective. Please understand that hiring practices is not an issue of affirmative action or preferential treatment, but more a matter of open-mindedness and intentionality. Pound for pound, talent for talent, you always want the best person on your team. The challenge is that if the only people on your team are those that look like you, chances are that you could suffer from a race complex. (Race complex: I only see things through the lens of my race. I desire to connect with, associate with, work with, and hire those people who look like me.)

Cafeteria Worker Syndrome

I remember when my oldest son Wesley was in the fifth grade, he asked me a question that jacked me up in a good way. He said, "Dad, why are the cafeteria workers at every one of my schools always black?" I had to pause and just let that roll around in my little ol' head for a while. That question made me pose a bigger question for organizations and for the Church specifically. "Are minorities only in 'cafeteria worker' positions at our church?" I'm not talking about cafeteria workers literally, but the spirit of moving toward having minorities represented at the highest levels of organizational leadership. Yes, your organization may have minorities represented, but are they represented at the highest levels of leadership? It's not acceptable in 2011 for churches and denominations to be content with minorities only being able to rise to the level of the cafeteria worker. *Cafeteria Worker Syndrome* is not about degrading the importance of the cafeteria worker or specific ministry roles, as all parts of the body are important. It's about recognizing that a diverse leadership team will make the cafeteria worker even better and communicate value and potential. Although this is more prominent in churches of the majority culture, it's not a predominantly white church thing only. This is something that predominantly African American, Asian, and Indian churches must wrestle with as well. Leaders and congregants, take a look at the leadership at the highest levels of your church and make a hard assessment. Can your church do better?

In chapter 2, I introduced Lee Rowland, who is the principal of Tulakes Elementary School. Lee is the only African American principal in Putnam City School District, and according to administrators that I've talked to, he may be the first African American to become a principal in the history of the district.

Congratulations to district leaders for making the decision to hire Lee. His leadership is impacting the lives of countless families and an entire community. You have to begin somewhere. Diversity change is something that takes time for certain communities and certain contexts. Start with the heart, and over time God will begin to create opportunities for growth and change. The church can't be an institution that settles for minorities only being able to be the cafeteria workers.

3. Does someone from the non-majority culture of my church share the pulpit? Does someone of the opposite race of the senior pastor or teaching pastor share the teaching responsibilities?

In the nine years I have been at LifeChurch.tv we have had Herbert Cooper (African American) teach twice, Francis Chan (Chinese American) once and Dr. Sam Chand (Indian) once, from a global perspective. Tome (South Tulsa) and I are able to teach to our individual campuses several times a year, and outside of that an ethnic minority has not shared the teaching responsibilities. This is definitely an area with room for growth in most churches around the country, including LifeChurch.tv. We have been fortunate to be voted the most innovative church in America several years in a row for the many great innovations that we have presented to the capital *C* Church. I pray that diversity in teaching will be another innovation that LifeChurch.tv will bring to the global Church, especially to the many ministry leaders around the globe that look to LifeChurch.tv for inspiration and innovation.

Willingness to share the teaching responsibilities with a minority is the ultimate church diversity litmus test for any church or ministry leader. Am I able to share the pulpit and teaching responsibilities with a minority or someone who doesn't look like, act like, or even teach like me? If you have capable leaders within your church or peer group, utilize them. Otherwise you may have to bring in a guest speaker. I think the minimal amount of time that a ministry should bring in a minority guest speaker is twice a year. There are many great communicators in your area and even more that are a phone call away. This assessment process allows those ministries that may be located in an area that doesn't have much diversity to develop a relationship with a ministry across town that may be facing the same challenges. A swapping of pulpit relationship fills a couple of the natural church diversity voids. Congregations are exposed to an entirely different ministry and begin to see someone that doesn't look like them in their pulpit. Again, having a church receive biblical instruction, teaching, correction, and leadership from a minority speaks volumes. The teaching duties or "the pulpit" is generally the last thing that a pastor will give up and the most difficult facet of diversity for the majority culture to receive. We can't underestimate the value of the teaching, due to the fact that teaching is the critical aspect in guiding and setting direction from the Church.

Not only should the church have diversity in the teacher, the senior or teaching pastor should teach on diversity, racial reconciliation, everyone being welcome, or something similar. This type of teaching will help establish a culture of diversity as a value and will create a spark in the hearts of the people.

James 3:1–5 outlines the power of teaching and what can happen as a result of it: "Not many of you should become teachers, my fellow believers, because you know that we who teach will be judged more strictly. We all stumble in many ways. Anyone who is never at fault in what they say is perfect, able to keep their whole body in check. When we put bits into the mouths of horses to make them obey us, we can turn the whole animal. Or take ships as an example. Although they are so large and are driven by strong winds, they are steered by a very small rudder wherever the pilot wants to go. Likewise, the tongue is a small part of the body, but it makes great boasts. Consider what a great forest is set on fire by a small spark." Teaching on diversity and having diversity in those providing the teaching helps to define the culture and guide the ship. A great barometer for a ministry to evaluate whether they are teaching on diversity enough is this: teach on diversity within any given calendar year the same number of times that you teach on giving. Who is teaching next week? What are they talking about?

4. Does my church have an overall culture of embracing diversity? This is the all-encompassing question. This question is the one that forces you to look at everything, and leads to more specific questions.

- Is diversity a core value or part of our ethos?
- Is Martin Luther King Jr. Day recognized as an official holiday for our church? (Basic litmus test for having an identified culture that embraces diversity.)
- Are print and media materials diversity sensitive?
- Is our platform diverse?
- How many times have I heard the "D-Word" (diverse or diversity) in the last year? Some people prefer multiethnic as their descriptor.
- Is there diversity in our music?

The list of questions goes on and on. This is the general assessment process of looking at your church through diversity lenses and an overall diversity grid. Does your church have a sign on the door that reads EVERYONE WELCOME? Everything you do, as well as the things you decide not to do, answers that question.

Martin Luther King Day (MLK Day)

MLK Day is a holiday that has been riddled with controversy since its inception. The voting process for passage of the bill to honor MLK Day was met with strong opposition. The bill was first submitted in 1979, signed into law by President Reagan in 1983, and first observed in 1986. South Carolina was the last state to honor MLK Day as an official state holiday, in May 2000.

Here we are, 25 years since the establishment of MLK Day and similar disagreement, opposition, and controversy still exists. Unfortunately, these disagreements still exist among ministry leaders, more so than government and corporate America, as most government agencies have honored MLK Day for years. This isn't meant to be divisive between those churches that honor the holiday and those that do not. For some reason, many ministry leaders and churches remain behind the curve on observation of MLK Day, and in my opinion, they should be the catalytic leaders touting the importance.

As ministry leaders begin to look for low-hanging fruit to begin the process of embracing church diversity, observation of Martin Luther King Jr. Day is a great place to start. I mentioned previously that sharing the pulpit and teaching responsibilities is the *ultimate* litmus test for embracing diversity; honoring MLK Day is the *basic* litmus test. This is seriously a no-brainer — a federal holiday that schools and businesses around the country already observe. Observing MLK Day as an official holiday has implications for not only the staff, but for the overall congregation as well. Imagine the senior pastor, campus pastor, or whoever does the announcements communicating something as simple as this: "Our offices will be closed Monday in honor of Martin Luther King Jr. holiday. He was a great man of God, a pastor and a great visionary; it's our honor to be closed in observance of MLK Day." Or, "Our offices will be closed on MLK Day. Many of you will have children who will be home from school that day. Take some time to share with your children the importance of Martin Luther King Jr.'s contribution to our nation and the global church." It doesn't matter how you say it — just understand that a couple of sentences can communicate a thousand words.

For those who argue that the church being closed on MLK Day is somehow disrespecting Martin Luther King Jr., I would ask the question, "Is it disrespectful to the Declaration of Independence to close in honor of the fourth of July?" I'd say absolutely not. There are plenty of options to have prayer meetings, days of service, and countless other creative ways to honor the holiday. I think what a ministry chooses to do on the holiday is an evolutionary process. The most important aspect is to observe the holiday and close the doors.

I remember doing some consulting with a multisite, multiethnic mega church and having conversations about MLK Day. I had mentioned that it would be very difficult for a church such as theirs to not honor MLK Day. As soon as I said those words the room got as quiet as a church mouse. There were some clear frustrations with the lack of observance. I met privately with the senior pastor the next day and he stated, "I didn't even think about it. That is definitely something that we will change."

Our actions will always be judged one way or the other. People outside of your church whom you are hoping to bring inside of your community will judge you by what you have done and what you celebrate. My personal opinion is that honoring MLK Day can be a win-win for any ministry, no matter the community.

There are varying opinions on this subject and many people don't feel that the church should be closed for such a holiday. Often times the argument is *We don't even close our church on Easter or Christmas*. In my opinion, that's comparing apples to oranges. Christmas and Easter are the two largest attended days of the year and MLK Day is on a Monday. I'm not talking about the weekend or mid-week church services, I'm talking about Monday, the holiday.

Others will pose the question, *Why should we honor MLK by shutting down?* I would answer that question this way: it's already been established as a federal holiday, schools are closed, banks are closed, government offices are closed, and in my opinion, churches should be closed. Again, this is the lowest-hanging fruit and an easy opportunity for ministry leaders to communicate that diversity and civil rights matter to their church. It puts the values that MLK stood for on the hearts of the congregation when ministry leaders remind them they will be closed. It softens the hearts of the staff by allowing them to reflect on the importance and understanding that diversity is a value. Seriously, I could go on and on. The bottom line is that not honoring MLK Day could potentially communicate a negative message to congregants, staff, or the community and honoring communicates a positive message. Therefore honoring MLK-Day is a win-win. The church should be at the forefront on issues of embracing the "everyone welcome" message that MLK died for, not the government, banking industry, education system, or corporate America. Yes, I will frequent a sandwich shop or business that's open on MLK Day. Those sandwich shops are not called to be the hope of the world and make disciples . . . they make sandwiches.

It doesn't matter if you choose to personally honor MLK Day by attending the local MLK Day Parade, serving in the community, watching old speeches, sharing history, praying, or reflecting with your family. Do something, because our culture is getting removed from historic realities year after year. MLK Day is a day to celebrate equality, diversity, and what the church should be leading — social justice. It's not merely about MLK the man, but rather the federal holiday in honor of what the man, his ministry, and his life stood for — what he died for.

Church Diversity Week

Church Diversity Week will be a globally recognized week to encourage and promote unity within the local church. It will begin on the second Friday of January and end on the third Friday of January each year. This week happens to fall on the calendar beginning the Friday prior to Martin Luther King Jr. Day (MLK Day) and lasts the entire week. There are many different ways to celebrate Church Diversity Week; however, at its core it's about encouraging and promoting unity and diversity in the Church. See the appendix for details and celebration suggestions.

Believe

The process of *believe* is a two-way street — believing and being believable. Once you believe, it's much easier to cast a vision of those beliefs and then and only then will you be able to truly inspire others. Here are some common phrases used among ministry leaders regarding vision casting: you can't lead your church to give if you are not giving; you can't lead your church to serve if you are not serving; you can't lead your church to worship if you're not worshiping; etc. The essence of these statements is the fact that you can't successfully lead your people to a place that's not a value of yours. You can't lead your church to embrace a culture of diversity if you don't *believe* that it's important and embrace a culture of diversity in your own life. It is more than just saying you want a few black volunteers, staff members, or attendees. It's the heart of "I *believe*" diversity that really matters.

As a ministry leader *I believe* that having a heart that embraces diversity is one piece of the puzzle to reach the world for Christ. I have to believe it and I have to live it. Bishop T.D. Jakes charged 13,000 ministry leaders with his own version of "Believe It and Live It" when he delivered a powerful future-focused message of hope at the 2010 Catalyst Conference. In a portion of his message Bishop Jakes said it this way:

> Are we armed with the language that reaches the masses? Or are we armed with the language and the subtle message that alienates the world? The disciples had the real challenge of taking what happened on the Cross and presenting it into the world. So they wrote books where they defied culture and went in to change the world, books like Romans and Hebrews and Ephesians. Those books indicate how the Church leaped over walls and went out there to do something awesome. A lot of leaders want to something awesome in the world, they want to touch the world and they want to win the world. They want to reach everybody! But you can't be multicultural and reach the world if you're not a multicultural person. You have to run the risk of bringing people into your life, and learn from them, not just into the Church. You can't stage people like props in your church and alienate them out of your life. You gotta sit down and eat some chicken, find out what collard greens are and potato salad. You got to go down to Mexico and eat some Mexican food.
>
> If you always do what you've always done, you'll always be where you've always been, and you can congratulate yourself for doing a good job. But if you do the good job in a fish tank, but you're called to an ocean, what are you missing? Do you know fish grow to the size of the tank you put them in? You put them in a small tank, they won't get real big. You put them in a big tank, they'll keep growing and growing. God wants you in the ocean.

I *believe* that God wants to expand our horizon and broaden our reach. We have been swimming around in the limited waters of segregated churches. Pastors, God doesn't want you to sprinkle a little fish food into the top of your little fish tank, but rather expand the food that you share to an ocean. There are a lot of hungry fish of all different colors, but we can't reach them with the living water if we are swimming around in our segregated fish tanks. Not only are we unable to reach the masses, but our potential for growth is stunted. It's time to start emphatically believing. It's time to change the waters; it's time to change the world.

Change

The South

I remember the first time I shared the concepts from this book in a live audience setting. I was invited to speak at The Sticks Conference in Orangeburg, South Carolina, in November of 2010. As I previously mentioned, The Sticks is a conference for those in small- to medium-sized towns who have tremendous passion, insight, leadership, and knowledge to reach areas of the country no one else dares to reach. It's for those ministry leaders leading in rural America, a.k.a. "The Sticks." This was an amazing opportunity to share a message with ministry leaders who really needed to hear it. Many of them were from communities in the "South" where serious racial tensions existed and remnants still remain. The South, "deep South" or "dirty South" as some like to say, is a term of endearment for the area of the United States that includes much of the former Confederacy, including Virginia, North Carolina, South Carolina, Georgia, Florida, Tennessee, Alabama, Mississippi, Louisiana, Arkansas, and Texas.

To be honest, I wasn't sure how rural pastors in the South would receive the church diversity message. But it was very well received and I had person after person come share with me stories of how they believed that this was an important message for their community. Several shared that the message forced them to deal with their own prejudice and confront a community history of segregation and racism. I had the opportunity to visit with one senior pastor, Chad Hunt, from the rural community of Cave City, Kentucky. Chad leads Caveland Church, which is a contemporary church of around 500 people in a community of less than 2,000. According to Chad, you have the "white church" and the "black church" in the rural Kentucky community. Chad said the church diversity message that I shared really struck a chord with him and he truly *believed* that it was time for him and his church to do something about it.

Chad had assessed where he and his church were and began to believe that the church diversity message mattered to God and therefore mattered to him. He *believed* that "doing something about it" was simply the right thing to do. I had several phone, e-mail, and social media conversations with Chad over the next month or so. When a senior leader believes in the heart of this message, change will happen and it will happen quickly. During one phone conversation I had with Chad, he informed me that he had rolled out the vision to make diversity a value in his church. He informed me that he stood up in a pulpit with an African American member of his church and stated that Cave City or

"Caveland" is going to be diverse. He said he received mixed reviews, but most were positive. He also responded publicly to the negative e-mails that he received the following week and informed his congregants that if they had a problem with it they were racist and needed to repent, and if they didn't like it they could leave. Whoa! That's called assessing, believing, and changing. I don't recommend Chad's exact approach for everyone, or you might lose your entire church. On the other hand, that's exactly what some congregations need to hear. When the senior pastor believes in the church diversity message, it's very easy for them to be authentic and believable to their congregation. When you believe, change is just around the corner.

Change always seems to be the most difficult part of moving people from where they are to where they need to be. I remember my days as a 20-some-thing-year-old warden taking over a new prison. The prison wasn't new in age, but rather new to me. A very old-guard prison warden had previously operated this particular prison. He was stuck in a leadership chasm that was no longer effective — I'm not sure if it ever was. The first thing I did was to begin making the necessary changes for the inmates and staff. I began walking my staff through the book and training video from Dr. Spencer Johnson's bestselling book *Who Moved My Cheese?*[1] This book has a simple concept about mice and cheese. Although the book was written in 1998, in my opinion, it's the best book about the understanding and application of change that I've read. As we began to make the necessary changes, it was difficult at first. Initially, staff and inmates were both skeptical and somewhat resistant to the change recommendations and implementations. In a short period of time, however, we totally changed the culture of this prison facility. When my tour of duty at this facility was complete and I was on my way out, the staff wrote me letters and cards. The majority of the cards focused on the positive change they were a part of, and many of them even shared illustrations from *Who Moved My Cheese?*

As we are all to be active diversity change agents for God's house, we must know that people will be resistant and skeptical in the beginning. Once change begins to happen and we help the Church glance into the future, we are one step closer to the change becoming a lasting reality. Latino civil rights activist Cesar Chavez articulates it in this manner, "Once social change begins, it cannot be reversed. You cannot uneducate the person who has learned to read. You cannot humiliate the person who feels pride. You cannot oppress the people who are not afraid anymore. We have seen the future, and the future is ours."[2] Years from now, Christians will write letters, books, blogs, and social media updates pointing to a time period when God's people began a biblical movement of social and heart change for the Church. A movement that changed the world.

Protect Your Blind Side

What happens when we Assess → Believe → Change? We move from where we are to where we need to be. When we get out of our comfort zones and go across the diversity tracks of life, our perspective changes. If we change our perspective, we change the game. Eyes are opened when Christians get out of their comfort zones, culture, history, and ways of doing church. I thought the blockbuster movie *The Blind Side* provided an excellent illustration of the change that happens if the Church will simply get off the sidelines of diversity and get in the game.

In the movie *The Blind Side*, Sandra Bullock plays the role of Leigh Anne Tuohy. The Tuohys are a white Christian family led by wealthy restaurant chain owner Sean Tuohy, played by Tim McGraw. The short and skinny on the movie is that an African American young man (Michael Oher aka Big Mike) from the other side of the tracks gets a shot to attend a rich private school, the Tuohys adopt him, he learns how to read, gets his grades up, becomes an excellent right tackle, learns to protect the quarterback's blind side, goes on to play college ball at Ole Miss, and eventually gets drafted in the 2009 NFL by the Baltimore Ravens.

There were several scenes in the movie where Leigh Anne Tuohy was heart-broken by what she experienced in "the Hood," an area that she never realized existed only 20 minutes from her beautiful suburban home. She had a desire to reach out, give, and make a difference. I vividly remember the scene where Leigh Anne confronted some of her rich, swanky girlfriends about their nega-tive stereotypes as she had a desire to connect with and change a community that she never knew existed. Leigh Anne's girlfriend asked, "Is this some sort of white guilt thing?" Leigh Anne responds by saying, "I don't need you all to approve my choices, but I do ask that you respect them. You have no idea what that boy has been through and if this is going to be some running diatribe, I can find an over-priced salad a lot closer to home." Her friend responds with, "Leigh Anne, I'm so sorry, I think what you are doing is so great, to open up your home to him. . . . Honey, you're changing that boy's life." Leigh Anne closes with, "No, he's changing mine!" She then immediately gets up and leaves. Leigh Anne's perspective had changed. *Change your perspective. Change the game. The Blind Side* has changed the game for the millions of people that watched the movie. The movie will impact generations to come. Small pushes over time result in big changes.

Still Dreaming

In November of 2010, I had the opportunity to speak at a Micro-Conference for Executive Leaders in Memphis, Tennessee. This conference was put on by City Leadership-Memphis and was a roundtable-type setting with about 15 to 20 leaders from a wide range of churches. I was one of the featured speakers along with Pastor John "J.B." Bryson (Fellowship Memphis, featured in chapter 6), and Pastor Josh Patterson (Village Church). We had an amazing couple of days of sharing, listening, and learning. Memphis is a city with such history. Issues of race and diversity always seemed to be front and center. Before going to the airport, John Caroll, who co-leads City Leadership, gave us a tour of Memphis. We were able to tour the area where "Big Mike" from the movie *The Blind Side* lived before a gentrification process happened. (Gentrification is the process of renewal and rebuilding accompanying the influx of middle-class or affluent people into deteriorating areas that often displaces poorer residents.) Talk about living and breathing diversity — John lived it. John was a white guy, lived in a predominantly black community, and he and his wife had two adopted black kids. The community was called "Uptown," formerly known as "Hurt Village" or "Big Mike's hood" before gentrification.

The highlight of our tour was getting to stop by the National Civil Rights Museum, which was birthed out of the success of the civil rights movement and the tragic violence that occurred at the Lorraine Motel, where Dr. Martin Luther King Jr. was assassinated. The museum is actually connected to the Lorraine Motel and the vehicles have been restored and maintained out in front of the motel. The motel also keeps rooms 306 and 307 as shrines. Room 307 is the last room Dr. King was in before he was assassinated outside of room 306. Room 306 was the room that Dr. King would frequently stay in during his visits.

As I peered up at the balcony, I began to imagine what was going through the mind of this civil rights leader before he was assassinated. He was in town on business, the business of helping the black sanitation workers who were striking for job safety, better wages and benefits, and union recognition. Dr. King was the most public "Do the Right Thing Leader" in the last century, in my opinion. His efforts were always selfless and he was always willing to put his life on the line for what was right. The reality is, I might not have been able to type these pages if it wasn't for Dr. King and others like him. We would never be able to have discussions about God's house being integrated, because segregation would be forced and fine by most. As Christians we have none of the barriers that Dr. King had, and yet we choose to put up self-imposed roadblocks between ourselves and what's right.

Dr. King is known for many accomplishments, demonstrations, and speeches. None were more famous than his "I Have a Dream" speech, a 17-minute public speech that Dr. King eloquently delivered, in which he called for racial equality and an end to discrimination. King's delivery of the speech on August 28, 1963, from the steps of the Lincoln Memorial during the March on Washington for Jobs and Freedom was a defining moment of the American Civil Rights Movement. King delivered this speech to a diverse group of over 200,000 civil rights supporters. The speech has had a lasting impact and was ranked the top American speech of the 20th century by a 1999 poll of scholars of public address. Many of you may be familiar with the portion of the speech where Dr. King states, "I have a dream that my four little children will one day live in a nation where they will not be judged by the color of their skin, but by the content of their character." Although that portion of the speech is important to the overall diversity discussion and church diversity dialogue, I'd like to share the closing words of the speech, to challenge the church, ministry leaders, denominations, and Christians-at-large to move from where they are to where they need to be.

The Church is in bondage to separatism and it's time to be *free*. The Church will be *free* in the same manner communicated in these closing words of Dr. King's "I Have a Dream" speech: "And when this happens, when we allow freedom to ring, when we let it ring from every tenement and every hamlet, from every state and every city, we will be able to speed up that day when all of God's children, black men and white men, Jews and Gentiles, Protestants and Catholics, will be able to join hands and sing in the words of the old Negro spiritual, 'Free at last, free at last. Thank God Almighty, The Church is free at last.'"

Dream BIG, Think BIGGER

One of my mantras is *dream BIG, think BIGGER* — as a matter of fact, it's the tagline on my blog BigIsTheNewSmall.com. It simply outlines the fact that thinking is the next step after dreaming and is the action step of making your dreams reality. Dr. King and countless others have dreamed for our world to look different, be different, and think different. We can't simply dream about change; we have do the hard work to make those dreams become an accomplished reality. *"Therefore, since we are surrounded by such a great cloud of witnesses, let us throw off everything that hinders and the sin that so easily entangles. And let us run with perseverance the race marked out for us"* (Hebrews 12:1).

I'll close with a thought from an excerpt of an old Apple commercial that aired years before the iMac, iPhone, or iPad popularity. The commercial challenged people to "think different." The grainy black and white commercial was one minute long. It featured footage of 17 iconic 20th century personalities; some living, others deceased. Those "dream BIG, think BIGGER" personalities included Albert Einstein, Bob Dylan, Martin Luther King Jr., Richard Branson, John Lennon (with Yoko Ono), Buckminster Fuller, Thomas Edison, Muhammad Ali, Ted Turner, Maria Callas, Mahatma Gandhi, Amelia Earhart, Alfred Hitchcock, Martha Graham, Jim Henson (with Kermit the Frog), Frank Lloyd Wright, and Pablo Picasso. The commercial ended with an image of a young girl opening her closed eyes, as if to see the possibilities before her.

The words of the commercial are as follows. Please read them through the lens of what it means to be a disciple of Christ, a "do the right thing leader," and a world changer. *"Here's to the crazy ones. The misfits. The rebels. The troublemakers. The round pegs in the square holes. The ones who see things differently. They're not fond of rules. And they have no respect for the status quo. You can quote them, disagree with them, glorify or vilify them. About the only thing you can't do is ignore them. Because they change things. They push the human race forward. And while some may see them as the crazy ones, we see genius. Because the people who are crazy enough to think they can change the world, are the ones who do."*[3]

I think we can change the church. I think we can change the world.

Dream BIG, think BIGGER.

 ## CHURCH DIVERSITY CHALLENGE 8

- Ask yourself the three personal assessment questions regarding diversity in your life. Based upon your answers, how would you rate yourself in terms of how well you embrace diversity in your relationships and in the way you think? Where do you need improvement?
- Ask yourself the four church assessment questions. Based upon your answers, how would you rate your church in terms of how well it exhibits a culture of embracing diversity? Where does your church need improvement?
- What do you believe when it comes to diversity in your church? What shifts in your beliefs do you need to make in order to become the catalyst that will enact change within your church?
- Based upon your assessment and your current beliefs, what specific changes do you need to enact within yourself and in your church to embrace a culture of diversity? How will you go about making these changes?

- What is your dream for diversity in your life and in your church? How will making that dream become a reality impact you, your church, and those you influence?

Endnotes

1. Spencer Johnson, *Who Moved My Cheese?* (New York: Putnam, 1998).
2. Cesar Chavez, address to the Commonwealth Club in San Francisco, Nov. 9, 1984, http://www.goodreads.com/author/quotes/345121.Cesar_Chavez.
3. "Apple Think Different" (YouTube video).

References

Books

Collins, James C. *Good to Great: Why Some Companies Make the Leap — and Others Don't.* New York: HarperBusiness, 2001.

Hybels, Bill. *Courageous Leadership.* Grand Rapids, MI: Zondervan, 2009.

Johnson, Spencer. *Who Moved My Cheese?* New York: Putnam, 1998.

Newman, Joe. *Race and the Assemblies of God Church.* Youngstown, NY: Cambria Press, 2007.

Stetzer, Ed, and David Putman. *Breaking the Missional Code.* Nashville, TN: Broadman & Holman, 2006.

Websites

"Apple Think Different" (YouTube video).

Bible Study.org: http://www.biblestudy.org/bibleref/meaning-of-numbers-in-bible/10.html.

Chavez, Cesar. address to the Commonwealth Club in San Francisco, Nov. 9, 1984, http://www.goodreads.com/author/quotes/345121.Cesar_Chavez.

Christianity Today. http://www.christianitytoday.com/ct/2005/april/23.36.html.

Diversity Inc. information, survey data, and quotes at http://www.diversityinc.com/pages/DI_50.shtml?id=7617.

My Play: http://myplay.com/artists/israel-houghton/bio.

TIME Magazine, "Can Mega Churches Bridge the Racial Divide?" http://www.time.com/time/magazine/article/0,9171,1950943,00.html.

United States Conference of Catholic Bishops. http://www.usccb.org/comm/archives/2010/10-040.shtml.

http://articles.orlandosentinel.com/2010-01-16/features/os-mlk-church-segregation-20100116_1_segregated-dr-king-race-or-ethnicity.

http://www.purposedrivenlife.com/en-US/FreeTools/devotional/dailyDevotional.htm.

http://www.mlkonline.net/christians.html.

www.stevenfurtick.com

We Are Church Diversity! Each Twitter name below represents someone who submitted their photo as a personal endorsement of ethnic diversity within the Church. Connect with them and @ScottWilliams at churchdiversity.com to continue the conversation.

@jenniferowhite
@samchacko
@kevindeshazo
@gmtaylor42141
@SpanishJedi
@showmeokc
@jerryGodsey
@rebeccagood
@davesears
@dustinkipe
@ales
@Decide2day
@key2texas2009
@rt44man
@estreitta
@epicparent
@charleskc
@nilwona
@Rami_rodz
@timdruhym
@thompsonland
@Bukker1
@jeremy_chandler
@idamrivera
@nanpalmero
@Bobinbama
@tristaanogre
@TubsWife
@jpierce757
@dannywahlquist
@marielle116
@dannyjbixby
@josephdpayne

@tricialovejoy
@preist
@marcmillan
@CarloSer
@desiwright
@navets
@blessingmpofu
@TheJohnsFamily
@laurynw
@thepaulellis
@freduhl
@StevenRossYoung
@artiedavis
@kylereed
@beth_bates
@ronedmondson
@jasonyounglive
@edgarcabelllo
@michele07
@heredes
@marcyr
@sarahfholbrook
@drfaithabraham
@_jessicawoods
@jdeddins
@tijuanabecky
@brandiereisman
@lbran
@lonerangerone
@tedrickdh
@deusami
@darrenemory
@thejanellekeith

@michaelhsmith
@stacyhag
@traceyknits
@BrianVasil
@roccocapra
@glynis_crawford
@revzed
@davidpepplersr
@froc
@grip
@jondunn8
@coachchristine
@sundijo
@revtrev
@joshbrickey
@jmarrapodi
@marblefamily
@JCWert
@terriknoll
@matthowden
@tallyrich
@CTopher81
@brownmantx
@erikagordon
@erinbbird
@ebroussard
@BrentFoulke
@chrishennessey
@timjchambers
@kylewsmith
@EstherRennick
@alandanielson
@davebaldwin

@andrealschultz
@iChilly
@mattgrube
@TheresaTrotter
@yochanan
@dazpacket
@handmaiden555
@johndobbs
@kend
@duongsheahan
@theblanchard
@CyndiAKADisneyq
@therichieallen
@derwinlgray
@Cheery01
@robrash
@LeadHership
@marvinlwilliams
@captianhavens
@healingimpact
@lolitawrites
@philgerb
@rlscovens
@melmasengale
@exodus195
@eddyau
@levittmike
@PastorRuss09
@chadstutzman
@ouharleyman
@ryan_garcia
@cwileygo
@mackinnonchris

@bsoist
@terracecrawford
@secondchair
@kenny_elliott
@sarnaa
@churchmediaguy
@DonaldOhse
@neosoul
@PastorTonyMoore
@greggackle
@mikebonedesign
@unscriptedlife
@rkinnick59
@jermyreeves
@robspeaks
@DannyLYoungers
@smalltownpastor
@chrislockemy
@mikemyatt
@girlnamedmeg
@small_Words
@mbstockdale
@jeremymoore
@juanmarketing
@redhedrev
@marshalljonesjr
@pmjlmj7380
@stellabonita
@tragic_pizza
@jerburroughs
@pjon
@TamiHeim
@JimmyHankins
@alyro
@patrickcmoore
@trentdugas

@deandeguara
@sharieng
@mkaigwa
@djchuang
@wryanmelson
@gregatkinson
@civilque
@toddruth
@mrjacebreeback
@joe_sewell
@theWeir
@lanceloves
@VicktoryManuel
@kacibaldwin
@tarsnoe
@godsoverflow
@chrisdenham
@pwilsonjr
@fmonehin
@apichea
@ShelleyHendrix
@alonsito
@scottmo
@arkansite
@rachaelkbrown
@turnedout
@olgunny1980
@CWest28
@rfbryant
@bobinbama
@jodyearley
@helloheady
@chadmissildine
@JaysonJohn
@yperez43
@johncarroll77

@pastortomjam
@willieharris
@mikefoster12
@gianniduarte
@rami_rod
@austinkoehn
@chazzdaddy
@Amart62
@exodusmovement
@yaminnette
@Mpowered64
@blakeporter
@lyndseybo
@caspergrl
@tonywinkler
@inworship
@miller_schloss
@DeniseWBarreto
@rachelleizard
@nycpastore
@MikeSingletary
@helenleeauthor
@HethieBaby
@erinbar
@Darlene_Kelley
@jsym
@matthewsloop
@brittneypirtle
@michaelscoleman
@lakendria
@rachellerm
@loretta ringo
@dontebee
@justinsrefuge
@KristenTeaff
@mgallops

@Soar_Coaching
@delamora
@holyghostaholic
@jbledsoejr
@seangosnell
@headphonaught
@stepanana
@_natewoods
@obedthomas
@scerny
@TheHubbz
@cameronthubbard
@sonnylemmons
@austinkoehn
@jessica_larson
@yami62
@Ttime710
@jrichardbyrd
@saltminepastor
@chadmckamie
@laryssatoomer
@jtoomer
@TwistedFelicity
@orionberridge
@cbran
@amyellacreative
@darrencurrin
@brightonrick
@Michael_Reece
@jasonshafer
@senorashafer
@jennifermle

Appendix

Church Diversity Week

As we seek to continue this conversation and begin to truly see signs on the doors of our church that read EVERYONE WELCOME, we want to provide a platform for churches to become a part of the movement. Church Diversity Week will begin on the second Friday of January each year. Suggestions for Church Diversity Week include but are not limited to:

- Teach unity, diversity, and inclusion in every service: worship, Sunday school, children's ministry, and student ministry.
- Do community service projects in conjunction with MLK Day.
- Swap pulpits with another pastor of a church with a different majority culture population.
- Allow a minority pastor to share the weekend message.
- Conduct online meet-ups and social media gatherings to discuss issues of diversity in the Church.
- Promote books, materials, and movies that promote a message of diversity in the Church.
- Work with media outlets to produce news stories about diversity in the Church.
- Write a letter to the editor of your local newspaper.
- Host a pastor's roundtable discussion in your local community.
- Involve your family and church in local MLK festivities.
- Share a story about "Everyone Welcome" or "Church Diversity" from your church (video or live).
- Inject creative elements promoting diversity into your drama and worship services.
- Share a Bible verse that encourages diversity in the Church or promote a daily Bible reading of specific verses during Church Diversity Week.
- Go to churchdiversity.com and buy the t-shirt, wear the t-shirt.
- Go to churchdiversity.com or churchdiversityweek.com and share your thoughts, ideas, and suggestions.

Diversity matters to God; the local church is the hope of the world. We *are* church diversity.

The inaugural Church Diversity Week will begin Friday, January 13th 2012 and will be every year thereafter. This week is dedicated to further the conversation and propel the movement to have a little heaven on earth.

Connect with New Leaf Publishing Group

facebook.com/**masterbooks**
twitter.com/**masterbooks4u**
youtube.com/**nlpgvideo**

nlpgblogs.com
nlpgvideos.com

join us at **Creation**Conversations.com